FIFTY RECIPES TO STAKE YOUR LIFE ON

Fifty Recipes To Stake Your Life On

A culinary memoir by
CHARLES CAMPION

TIMEWELL PRESS

First published in Great Britain in 2004 by
Timewell Press Limited
63 Kensington Gardens Square, London W2 4DG

ISBN 1 85725 202 0

Design by Sheila Thorpe. Typeset by Antony Gray
Printed and bound in Great Britain by
Biddles Ltd, King's Lynn

Contents

CONTENTS

To my wife
Sylvia
without whom
it would all be impossible

INTRODUCTION

You know what it's like: you go into the kitchen, pick up an oven glove, open the cooker door and aaargh . . . ! Then, if you're lucky, you wake up and sit shaking on the edge of the bed as it slowly dawns that the collapse of your dinner party was only a horrid nightmare. Or, alternatively, you look at the burnt offering in the oven in stunned disbelief and realise that it's only too real.

It's the same as that ghastly moment when you get into the car, turn the key and nothing – not a murmur, not a sound. Day in, day out, everything works perfectly well and then quite suddenly, and for no apparent reason, it doesn't. That wretched sinking feeling, and the rage that accompanies it, seems even worse when it is the recipe that has let you down – for once you have done everything according to the book but even then nothing has worked.

That won't happen with these recipes because all of these recipes work.

I have developed some, inherited others and refined them all. As any racing tipster will tell you, to be convincing any recommendation must come with its own individual story . . . so here you are: fifty, sure-fire, tried-and-tested recipes and fifty stories to go with them.

These dishes may not make as much impression on your guests as a perfect plateful of *haute cuisine*, but they will never let you down. In making an essentially personal choice, I have tried to include some more eccentric dishes, homespun dishes, flamboyant dishes, vegetarian dishes, family dishes, fattening dishes, slimming dishes – in fact a full armoury for busy cooks who have to entertain, feed the kids, splash out and cut back, as well as everything else.

Happy cooking!

Charles Campion

Worcester, 2004

Number One – Not Lardy Cake

*In which a little old lady from Wiltshire
locks horns with the Roux brothers*

For a long while I was sure that the finest lardy cake in all the world came from a baker in Cullompton High Street, Devon. It was a magnificent, sumptuous affair: golden, squelchy and riddled through with mixed fruit – including lots of tangy peel. A much grander creation than the traditional cake that started out as a sensible and cost-effective way of using up that last bit of bread dough. It hardly seems fair that a mythical little old Wiltshire lady with rosy cheeks, red hands and a floury pinafore should always get the credit for this classic English teatime treat. Nevertheless, by convention it is called 'Wiltshire' Lardy Cake (even in Jane Grigson's wonderful book *English Food*, and her scholarship is exemplary). Perhaps one day an earnest student will come up with a PhD thesis on the underlying links between the Wiltshire bacon industry and the lard required.

Lard's strange stuff. You'd put butter on toast, or dripping, or even modern cholesterol-lowering spreads, but you'd never chomp your way through a piece of toast and lard. Lard is the ultimate in heavy grease, giving substance to the fried bread in cafe fry-ups, the raw material of heart attacks. Moreover, lard is an astonishing 890 kcal per 100 g. (Yes; I'm afraid that's right, this isn't a typographical error.)

Anyway, through a mist of guilt, I always liked lardy cake – especially that king of cakes from the baker's in Cullompton. So as I was skimming some recipe books one day it suddenly struck me that there were many parallels between lardy cake and croissants. I know that this revelation may not exactly leap off the page for everyone, but study the two and you'll find that they're sisters under the skin. They're both made from a straightforward, yeast-raised dough with fat layered through it in the same fashion as puff pastry.

If you've followed the Roux brothers' recipe, which sets out in detail the sixteen stages and twenty-two hours needed to make a passable croissant, you'll know that there are one or two wrinkles that make the difference; but essentially croissants are French cousins of the lardy cake.

This was my starting point. What, I wondered, would happen if I made my lardy cake without lard? Butter might be nice instead, and what if I changed the mixed fruit in a lardy cake for some of those nice 'no-need-to-soak', already plump, dried apricots cut up into fine shreds?

The result is a triumph. Crisp and succulent as lardy cake, with the tang of the apricots balancing the soggy richness of the buttery dough. It really should carry a self-indulgence warning: easy to make, not expensive, and always certain of the great reception it deserves.

INTRODUCTION

First of all you need bread dough. Don't be frightened, making nice bread is a lot easier than organically-principled, home-baking earth mothers would have us believe. The key lies in buying 'strong white breadmaking' flour and not just using up whatever is in the cupboard. Look out for flour made from Canadian wheat, but failing the exotic, any supermarket flour labelled 'strong white breadmaking' will do fine. Real yeast seems to help too. Nearly every other recipe for home-baked bread will tell you carefully that reconstituted dried yeast is indistinguishable from real fresh yeast in the finished product, so it must be true. It just doesn't seem that way to me, unless you take extra care over the reconstitution process. I'd recommend going to a baker and buying 75–100 g (3 or 4 oz) of fresh yeast, taking it home and dividing it into portions of about 12 g (roughly half an ounce) each, wrapping each in a twist of clingfilm and popping them in the deep freeze. I use them straight from the freezer as described in the method that follows.

To make the kneading process easier I suggest that you make twice as much bread dough as you need for this cake, and use the other half to make some bread or to pop in the freezer for another day.

DOUGH INGREDIENTS

700 g (1 lb 9 oz) strong white breadmaking flour
450 ml (16 fl oz) half and half, cold milk and boiling water

2 x 12 g (½ oz) twists of fresh yeast from the freezer

1 heaped tsp of white sugar

½ a level tsp of salt

25 g (1 oz) unsalted butter – melted

METHOD FOR THE DOUGH

Put the flour in a large bowl. Put everything else into a jug and stir until it is all dissolved. Take a wooden spoon to start with, then use your hands and work the contents of the jug into the flour until you have a dough that leaves the sides of the bowl cleanly. Use your judgement and add a little more flour or a little more warm water if you need to, and carry on until the dough is dough-like! Once the dough is holding together well transfer it to a board and knead. This action is hard to describe, but it's very like what cats do on your knee when they're purring and content. As you work the dough you'll find that it becomes wonderfully springy and resilient: it really is a great feeling! When this happens you know that you are getting to the gluten in the flour. You want a good, springy dough, which will have taken about ten minutes. Wash the bowl, and butter the whole of its inside so that the dough doesn't stick, then shape the dough into a ball and put it back into the bowl, cover with some clingfilm and leave it in a warm place for a couple of hours or until doubled in size. Just abandon it and do something else.

Then take the (by now quite large) dough ball out and knead it once again to break up the larger bubbles within it and give it a uniform texture. Then cut it in half with a knife. Half goes for bread (perhaps the recipe for 'sesame and tomato bread' – Recipe 41 – will catch your eye), or into the freezer; the other half is for the cake.

Take the dough and a rolling pin and wrestle it out into a rectangle approximately 45 cm long by 30 cm wide and 3 cm or so thick (18 in x 12 in x 1½ in).

CAKE INGREDIENTS

150 g (5½ oz) 'no-need-to-soak' dried apricots cut into strips
   about 4 mm wide with the kitchen scissors
150 g (5½ oz) fine golden demerara sugar
150 g (5½ oz) unsalted butter

Treat the dough as you would puff pastry; spread a third of your butter over two thirds of the rectangle, then sprinkle on a third of the sugar and a third of the apricots. Fold the 'blank' third into the middle and then the final third in as well.

Rotate the slab through ninety degrees and use the rolling pin to spread it out into a longer rectangle as before. None of this has to be inch perfect as you're not making tiny bits of precision patisserie.

Then start again, covering two thirds of the dough rectangle with filling. You're finished when you've given the dough three 'turns' – incidentally this should mean your finished cake has twenty-seven layers.

At the end of the final turn tuck the flaps in underneath making the whole thing into a tidy parcel about 30 cm (12 in) long by 15 cm (6 in) wide by 10 cm (4 in) tall, and sit the whole cake in a well-buttered tin – the one you do the Sunday joint in will do well. Cover and put it to one side out of draughts and let it 'prove' for half an hour; it'll swell up in size and prove to you that the yeast is still alive. Then paint the top with beaten egg and put it into a pre-heated oven, about three quarters of the way up (you probably know your oven best, what its little foibles are; and which shelf is the happiest). The oven setting should be: between gas mark 4 & 5 / 350–375°F / 180°C. Take a look after thirty-five minutes. Your cake will probably be done after forty minutes, when it should be rich brown and crisp on top. Do not worry about the small ocean of melted butter it seems to be swimming in. Take the roasting tin out of the oven and let the cake cool, still in the tin, for ten minutes – by which time this butter will be magically re-absorbed into the bottom of the cake and it will be ready for a careful transfer to a large plate, where you should let it cool before you pounce.

Number Two – Fiercely Barbecued Lamb

*In which a method for maximising the crispy
bits is examined in depth*

I had a school friend who always used to clamour for the *dog piece*
whenever he had Sunday lunch at our house. The *dog piece* is that little
knuckly bit you get on the forearm end of a shoulder of lamb; the bit the
butcher helpfully swipes through with a cleaver. Presumably somewhere
in his background was a baronial hall with attendant wolfhounds or a
kennel full of well-bred golden retrievers, all of whom were waiting for
the pickings from the high table.

The Greeks do it too. I don't mean that the Greek islands are
overrun with massive Baskervillian hounds, but that they have a canny
appreciation of the finer things in life – the crispy bits. The crispy bits
come into their own when you taste that rarely sighted, glorious,
genuinely charcoal-grilled delight that is *souvlaki*. Not at all like the
oven-warmed, pallid, much-easier-to-produce-in-bulk for hen-parties-
on-a-spree imposter that is so often found under the name *kleftico* on
Greek Cypriot restaurant menus.

Souvlaki is a brilliant dish. Whilst we were busily consigning the knuckle ends of lamb joints to our pets, Greek cuisine was developing this juicy, smoky, crispy delight, and that's the starting point for 'fiercely barbecued lamb'. For once the secret doesn't lie wholly in being choosy about the meat. You needn't use only lamb from Soay sheep whose seaweed diet is said to give them a unique savour. The dish won't founder if you don't insist on organically raised 'happy' lamb. It would be great to use premium meats, but everything will be fine even if your leg of lamb was frozen some time ago on a New Zealand hillside.

Basically the dish works like this: you take your piece of lamb, spend quite some time and effort on preparing it, cook it quickly and fiercely and then squabble over the crispy bits.

Obviously the best means of cooking something fiercely is on an outdoor barbecue. But if you don't have one, or if the mood to try this dish sweeps over you in February – at the time when the spring lamb now makes its ever-earlier appearance – do not despair, this plan will work for anyone with a grill and an oven.

Do not be caught up by the mystique of 'barbecue-itus'; I recently spotted one of the leading supermarkets selling bags containing chips of American hickory wood for barbecues – pound for pound, this fuel cost roughly the same as sirloin steak! The way a barbecue adds such a delicious flavour is by cooking the meat in the smoke generated when its own juices hit the fire. That's why the fire has to be so hot, that is why it's invariably smoky, and that's why it tends to be an outdoor activity. What fuels the fire is of secondary importance; in fact, there is a traditional grill room in the heart of the Black Country where the meat is grilled over a huge, incredibly hot, coke fire. It works a treat – although a blast furnace like that needs a full-time stoker and might prove a little extreme for the average back garden.

INTRODUCTION

There are two stages to this operation: the first is the marinating and the second is the cooking. For four people you need one medium-sized leg of lamb, but if it's to be just one course of a dinner a slightly larger leg will probably feed six. This is one occasion when you can happily take the bone out yourself as your objective is merely a sheet of lamb meat and it does not matter how ragged the edges are. If you're not confident, however, make your butcher work for his money.

So, you've got a flat sheet of lamb meat; skin one side and lean meat the other. Ideally this should go into the marinade overnight, but if circumstances dictate otherwise you can get by with leaving it to soak for about four hours. As with most marinades this one contains some strong flavour; something acid to tenderise the meat, and some oil and sugar to promote the formation of the all-important crispy bits. You'll notice that there's no salt because it has a counter-productive toughening effect on raw meat. So remember to salt the meat well when actually cooking it.

INGREDIENTS FOR THE MARINADE

5 cloves of garlic, peeled and sliced thinly.

The leaves stripped from 5 large sprigs of fresh rosemary.

2 level tbs dried oregano.

3 level tbs dark-brown sugar.

1 tbs Worcestershire sauce.

6 turns of freshly ground black pepper.

250 ml (9 fl oz) ordinary red wine.

100 ml (3½ fl oz) good olive oil.

30 ml (1 fl oz) walnut oil.

Mix all the marinade ingredients thoroughly with a fork. Get a large, strong, plastic bag (your butcher can help you here), add the marinade, and the lamb. Then comes the delightful messy bit. Use your hands to rub the marinade into the lamb. Work it well in and then try and expel all the air before sealing up the bag and popping it into the fridge to think to itself and mend its ways.

COOKING

The next question you must ask yourself is, 'How do my guests like their lamb?' I have a friend whose idea of a perfect piece of lamb is to eat it so rare that a candle would do the cooking job for him. Because of the cooking method used for this dish you have the choice. Yes, you can have it pink inside with crispy bits outside; or grey in the middle with crispy bits outside. Thankfully you always get crispy bits.

First of all, an hour before you plan to cook, light your barbecue. You will need very hot, white embers to cook over, and getting the barbecue into that condition always takes much longer than you would expect. (The little-heeded first law of barbecuing states that 'the coals are always in perfect condition for you to start cooking just after you have finished grilling the last piece of meat'.)

So, half an hour after lighting the barbecue take the lamb out of the marinade. Save the marinade in a jug and place the lamb on a rack in a roasting tin in your oven which you have pre-heated to gas mark 5 / 375 °F / 180°C. Cook it for about twenty minutes if you want the end product red, thirty minutes for pink, forty-five minutes for well done. Then take the part-cooked joint out for finishing on the barbecue, salt it, get the grill close to the coals, pop it on and baste with reserved marinade, turning regularly. All barbecues and all ovens are different, so if you have any doubts try a practice run, you'll find you soon get the balance right between pre-cooking and finishing – the balance that delivers exactly the level of cooking you want together with plenty of crispy bits. If you haven't got a barbecue simply use your grill and remember to keep turning the meat.

When the meat is done to your satisfaction take it off the barbecue and let it rest on a board for twenty minutes before carving it into wedge-shaped slices so that each piece has a balance of crispy bits and meat. Set it off with a crunchy salad of some kind, and fresh bread.

Number Three – Singapore Noodles

In which we get to grips with
the inscrutable Orient

To give credit where credit is due, it was Brian Sayer's discovery. Long ago Brian ran a thriving graphics and photography business in Covent Garden, and in some pub or other he struck up a friendship with a dynamic young Chinese businessman. One thing led to another, and pretty soon a joint venture was being discussed. They decided that what London was crying out for was its own Chinese language newspaper; Brian's studio was to handle the artwork and the Chinese connections would cope with content and distribution. And as is the case with all such pipe dreams everybody would certainly end up rich. In the end nothing came of it, but somewhere along the line Brian got a personal introduction to a truly amazing Chinese restaurant.

There is a scurrilous, and cleverly fabricated, story that Brian wrote to Hong Kong ordering a complete font of Chinese type, so as to be well ahead with the newspaper project. This tale goes on to tell how, in due course, the three lorries turned up at his studio with the twenty-two thousand Chinese characters, each in a range of sizes. And how he then found that his entire premises weren't big enough to take the type alone, to say nothing of the machinery, and as a result he had to send it all straight back unopened! I'm sure this is not true. (Sometimes we don't realise how lucky we are that there are only twenty-six different letters to deal with in the English language.)

But to return to the subject in hand. The restaurant was a gem: it was located in a dingy side street in the heart of London's Chinatown, and its decor left everything to be desired. On the rear wall was a photographic mural depicting palm trees and white sand beaches; overhead was a frayed wisp of netting from which were suspended a selection of tomato-soup-orange plastic lobsters; and the gentlemen's toilet was within a plywood box built on to the side of the room – woe betide sensitive diners at the adjoining table.

The food, however, was exquisite. The restaurant opened at four in the afternoon and it closed at four o'clock the following morning. As far as I could tell the only people who ate there consistently, except for us, were off-duty waiters from other Chinese establishments. We used to roll up just after midnight and enjoy the house speciality which was 'baked crab in ginger and spring onions'. A whole crab was plenty for two and used to cost roughly the same as three pints of beer.

Unfortunately nobody can keep a secret, and a wave of success was followed by a management buy-out, demolition of the downstairs gents, and a complete redesign of the dining-room. Hey presto, the Fung Shing had become one of London's senior Cantonese restaurants. Everybody in this restaurant was interested in food, from management to waiters, and when you asked how things were done you got a straight answer. Their Singapore noodle was particularly delicious, and the recipe given here owes a great deal to their expertise. This is a class above the yellow stained, curry-powder-flavoured lumps that masquerade as Singapore noodle in so many Chinese restaurants, mainly because the genuine spiciness of the dish stems from fresh chillies rather than packets and potions. However, cooking from bottles is not frowned on as much by Chinese chefs as by French ones.

I remember asking a helpful waiter how a crisply memorable dish of 'greens in oyster sauce' was made. He replied with a grin, 'Very complicated – wilt the greens in boiling water, then mix up equal parts of bottled oyster sauce and sesame oil and pour over the greens.'

Not quite as inscrutable as those misspent years reading Charlie Chan novellas may have led us to expect.

INTRODUCTION

Before Chinese cooking there must be Chinese shopping. As well as your own researches at many of the excellent Chinese supermarkets that are springing up everywhere, I would commend Ken Hom's excellent book *Chinese Cookery*, even if you only go into a library and read the section on ingredients.

The fixed elements in this recipe are:

Fine rice noodles – also known as rice vermicelli, or possibly as rice sticks. They come dried in packets like miniature bales of hay and are almost pure white. They make a wonderful store cupboard staple; they're ridiculously easy to prepare and take up whatever flavours you put near them.

Superior soy. Superior soy is the lighter of the two soy sauces (the thicker one being called soy superior sauce to make everyone's life more complicated). You'll find that a litre of soy in a Chinese supermarket costs a fraction less than 200 ml does in an ordinary supermarket.

Sesame oil. The same observation applies: large bottles in Chinese supermarkets are priced at the same level as miniature ones in the ordinary supermarkets.

Rice wine. It comes in bottles that look like they've already done service holding Johnny Walker scotch, as indeed they may have done for all I know. The correct term is Shaohsing wine. Books will tell you that you can substitute dry sherry and, who knows, they may be right. I prefer not to.

A wok. Once again get yourself down to a Chinese supermarket, buy yourself one of their woks – a large black-iron hubcap with an 18-inch broom handle sticking out of it – it won't cost a fifth of the price of a smart non-stick frying pan.

The other elements of this dish are variable. So get shopping! With one proviso: if fresh water chestnuts are in season and you see some, snap them up. They are devils to peel but repay the endeavour, tasting magical – hot, and sweet, and crisp, all at the same time – completely unlike their pallid cousins which masquerade in tins under the same name.

INGREDIENTS – per big dishful (a complete supper for two)

1 250 g packet of rice vermicelli
50 ml (2 fl oz) groundnut oil
25 ml (1 fl oz) sesame oil
100 ml (3½ oz) superior soy
4 cloves of garlic
1 bunch of spring onions
6 fresh green chillies

Then choose the five things you most like on the following list. Try to balance crisp with soft textures, sweet things with salty things, vegetables with meat or fish and so on. Use about 100 g (3½ oz) of each one you choose.

Pine kernels
Peanuts
Cashews
Chopped Chinese sausage

Shredded slice of your leftover Sunday joint

Sliced crisply fried bacon

Sliced carrot

Sliced fresh water chestnuts

Bean sprouts

Chinese greens – choi sum, pak choi

Frozen peas

Sweetcorn

Peeled prawns

Cooked squid

Oysters, fresh or smoked

Mussels (fresh, frozen or tinned)

2 eggs (beaten, fried and sliced)

METHOD

Take your pack of noodles and put them in a large mixing bowl. Pour a kettle of boiling water over them and let them stand for two minutes and then drain in a sieve.

Prepare your primary ingredients and put them in small bowls ready. Chop the spring onions into 1 cm (¼ in) lengths. Take the seeds out of your green chillies and chop them across into slivers. Crush your garlic in a press.

Decide on your other five ingredients and get them chopped and prepared. Then you're ready for the off, and you'll be enjoying this dish within five minutes. Put the oils into your wok and bring them up to medium heat (between lukewarm and smoking). Add the garlic, spring onions and chillies and turn the heat down, stirring and cooking for a minute, so that the oil takes up the flavourings. Add the rice wine and the superior soy sauce, then add everything else but the noodles and stir until it is all warmed through.

Then take the noodles from the water and strain them, pop them into the wok with everything else, where they will soak up all the liquid. Keep the noodles on the move so that they don't stick and so that they're well mixed with the other ingredients. As soon as the dish looks homogeneous, and is heated through, serve and eat – trying all the while to look inscrutable despite the delightful tastes and textures.

Number Four – Kidneys in Mild Mustard Sauce

*In which a butcher in Buxton gets some
of the credit he deserves*

When my wife and I were hotel proprietors in Buxton we were lucky in many respects. In particular we looked out over one of the finest views imaginable, and we had a wondrous butcher. It's hard to know which left a more lasting memory. Sneaking out of the kitchen at the end of service on a summer evening to sit on the garden bench and look across the darkening valley had undeniable attractions. As did waiting until the guests checked out and then lazing in the bath *en suite* to our best room – the French windows of that bathroom could be thrown open on to the same countryside.

On the other hand there were Mr Mycock's kidneys. Well not exactly his; to be strictly accurate the kidneys belonged to his steers which remorselessly won him prize after prize at local fatstock shows.

Like all success, this brought attendant problems. On one occasion I had to take a dish of oxtail with spring vegetables off the menu because I couldn't find the oxtails anywhere in my meat order. It transpired that my oxtails were still attached to the cattle; the steers had won some highly prized cup or other, and had been kept waiting by the local paper's photographer whose duty it was to record this happy event. The Derbyshire paparazzi had been unavoidably delayed in a pub and the slaughterhouse had shut before they could get the beasts there.

You have to admire a man who can create an excuse like that. You have to admire his kidneys too. There comes an arbitrary point in a calf's life when overnight it is no longer a calf with virulently pricey veal kidneys, but an ox whose kidneys are much cheaper and only fit for pies. This strange edict has been set in stone by the powers that be, who threaten to swoop with draconian ferocity on anyone who sells even slightly senior bovine kidneys as veal. It also transpires that since this *when-is-a-calf-not-a-calf* timetable was established, new breeds have been introduced, and calf nutrition improved to such an extent that they are making market weights earlier and earlier.

What happens to the kidneys from those strapping young beasts, the ones that are a few days too old to be called calves? Well, in Buxton our butcher would set them aside and sell them to me at roughly a fifth of the price of veal kidneys. I would then trample on the letter of the law and dish them up in the restaurant as calf's kidney. And jolly nice they were; in fact I was even persuaded to grill one whole – leaving the middle raw and cold on instructions – for Michel Legrand who was staying with us and performing a new work at the Buxton Festival; he liked it so much that he rushed into the kitchen to give me a Gallic hug.

At this point I feel that I should stress that whilst I like most things cooked very rare, even *bleu*, a whole kidney with a raw middle and that taint of urine so admired by Leopold Bloom was a bridge too far for my palate.

But when cooked in this mild mustard sauce Mr Mycock's not-calves' kidneys were splendid. So if you have the benefit of any kind of relationship with your butcher, and perhaps more importantly if he kills his own meat, ask about the kidneys. Ask to see one. You can soon tell: it should be firm, shiny, and about a double handful in size (please bear in mind that I have pretty large hands); each of the nodules that make up the kidney should be no bigger than an apricot. If it is large, dark, chocolate brown, and looks and feels tough, then don't waste this splendid sauce on it; pay the huge amount of money required and buy veal kidneys – English generally have more taste to them than Dutch.

INTRODUCTION

Most of my recipes follow a general principle. Start with carefully selected ingredients that are of the highest possible quality (but not always bearing the highest possible price ticket) and then take care not to spoil them by overdoing the fussing around.

This recipe is a case in point. It involves kidneys and just three simple ingredients, plus salt and pepper. It's as delicious and sophisticated a plateful as you could hope to ask for seconds of. There are no mysteries of technique, just adjust every element until it is exactly as you would want it.

You will need to be careful in buying your mustard. I like the Moutarde de Bourgogne which comes from Taylor and Lake, but any wholegrain, fairly spicy French mustard will serve. Moutarde de Meaux in those stone jars with sealing wax around the top is very nice, but carries with it one drawback: I've not yet found a way to shatter the seal and make my way past the cork into the mustard without a few of the shards of red sealing wax finding their way into the mustard and thence to the final dish where they prove to be very visible indeed.

INGREDIENTS

> 110 g (4 oz) unsalted butter
> Allow 3 smallish kidneys for four; select them carefully as
>   discussed earlier
> At least 4 heaped tbs of wholegrain Moutarde de Bourgogne
> A 284 ml carton of double cream
> Salt and freshly ground black pepper

METHOD

Wash the kidneys and, taking a pair of kitchen scissors, go through the rather laborious procedure of snipping each of the small lobes of kidney away from the hard white core. You should end up with the kidney in nice forkable pieces and separated from the bits you don't require.

Take whichever of your frying pans is both large and reliably non-stick, then melt the butter in it cautiously – don't go mad and end up with a sticky glop. Add the kidneys and fry them gently. They firm up quite quickly, and in five minutes will be nearly cooked. Lift them out and keep warm in a dish while you deal with the sauce. Try to make sure that as much of the juice as possible stays behind in the pan. Add the mustard to the butter and juices remaining in the pan. Turn up the heat and start cooking off the mustard. Imagine that you are making a roux; in another role, each grain of mustard is the raw material for making mustard flour, so your roux will thicken up nicely as you cook. (It'll also pop and fizz a bit as whole grains explode, so don't worry!) Let the resulting paste down by reducing the heat and adding the cream, cook on slowly and add salt and pepper to taste. Remember that when you add the kidneys you'll be adding back more juice that has collected whilst they were standing so, if anything, leave the sauce on the thick side to compensate. Add back the kidneys and turn the heat up a little. Turn the kidneys to coat them, and when the sauce looks to be at the right consistency (i.e. when you look at them and want to eat them), serve quickly. A nice potato gratin on the side would turn this dish from stupendous to earth-shattering.

Number Five – Dill Parsnips

In which fine words butter some parsnips

There was a time when I would have subscribed to the view that the only way of enjoying parsnips was to eat them roasted to caramel crispness alongside a shoulder of lamb. As a vegetable I used to find them too sweet, too mushy and too bland. Nowadays I know better, and this dish takes those very qualities I despised and uses them as the basis of a very good vegetable dish indeed.

The key elements are dill, and an ongoing search to make life easier on us cooks. Anything, but anything, that can be prepared in advance and not suffer gets my vote. Because of its mushy, watery nature parsnip is the microwave's very best friend, so make this purée in good time, wash up the food processor, and keep your parsnips in a bowl under a saucer. When you want to serve them just microwave, stir and serve – no problem.

Dill is a great herb. It gets one of its first write-ups in a tenth-century manuscript by Archbishop Aelfric, and had probably been introduced to Britain by the Romans. Once here it made quite a name for itself as an universal baby comforter – the name dill is supposed to be derived from the Saxon word *dilla* meaning to lull. Anyway, by the Middle Ages, it had secured a place in most cottage gardens where it was planted as an antidote to witchcraft. Today the Scandinavians treat it as their signature herb, and most of us have enjoyed the role it plays in gravadlax, or dill-pickled salmon. Cooks face a choice between two kinds of dill: there's dill seed and dill weed. For this dish you need dill weed, as the delicate threads of dill add the only visual interest to what could so easily become a grey mush. The memory of school dinners has left indelible scars on the imaginations of British cooks, and one of the worst of these is an antipathy to any kind of puréed vegetable. And it's not only parsnips that suffer; what about puréed swede, or bashed neaps as the Scots perversely insist on calling it? There's nothing intrinsically unpleasant about the taste of swede provided you remember that you are cooking it for yourself. Yes, that's right, you're actually going to down a few forkfuls in person . . . Viewed from this perspective you might pick smaller medium-sized swedes to start with; trim away the rugged bits; cook it conscientiously; pop it in the food processor with best butter, some ground mace, some freshly ground black pepper, a carefully judged amount of salt – think of eating the mashed swede yourself, release those inhibitions and you are much more likely to create something delicious.

Try pumpkin, too (butter, black pepper and a bit more salt).

Try celeriac (cream, salt and black pepper).

Try sweet potatoes (butter, black pepper, salt, lemon juice).

Try mixing new combinations.

But first of all try dill parsnips, it'll give you the confidence you need to fall in love with root vegetables.

INTRODUCTION

This purée can be served piped into rosettes, in cocotte dishes, and all sorts of other ways but it is very hard to beat an honest spoonful. It has a good texture, it's almost fluffy, and the tiny threads of dill contrast well with the base colour of the parsnip.

As to the parsnips themselves, you need to buy parsnips that are old enough to taste of something, but not so old they're woody. You don't want nouvelle cuisine miniature vegetables and you don't want great titanic hawsers either. Be careful with the salting, i.e. leave it until you're making the purée and go gently; parsnips soak up salt and if you salt the cooking water heavily you can end up overdoing it.

INGREDIENTS

Take sufficient parsnips (you didn't think I was about to say how many did you? Only you know how many guests you've got coming. Be on the safe side, however, and do a few extra – this really is delicious and unusual!).

Sufficient double cream to raise an eyebrow.
Salt and freshly ground black pepper.
Dried dill weed.

METHOD

First peel your parsnips and cut out any very woody bits. Cook in unsalted boiling water until they are soft. Strain off the water and let them stand for a minute to steam and dry off. Pop them into the food processor and turn it up to full speed until you have the finest purée possible. Leave it running . . .

Add cream, salt and pepper to taste. Then add your dried dill weed. I prefer lots – three tablespoonfuls or more to a half-full food processor. How much you use is up to your tastebuds and trial and error. Decant the purée into a serving dish and leave it to stand – several hours if needs be. Before serving, heat it thoroughly in a microwave and stir.

You may never roast a parsnip again.

Number Six – Smoked Trout and Coriander Mousse

In which a dull stand-by calls on
help from the East

It's hard to think of anything that's taken more of a crash-dive down the exotica rankings than smoked fish. Once, smoked salmon was the luxury of luxuries; nowadays mackerel, trout, wild salmon, farmed salmon, sea-farmed rainbow trout, eel and even halibut all crop up smoked, sliced and pressed into plastic at the larger supermarkets.

Fish farming has a lot to answer for. What else could the poor farmer do with an overproduction of twelve-ounce rainbows? To the smokehouse with them straightaway, and don't waste all that time and weight by cold smoking. Hot-smoke them and be quick about it. After all, there's always that American invention – 'smoke in a bottle' – which you can paint on for a truly authentic taste.

No wonder subtle smoked salmon and delicate smoked trout are now so hard to find. At this point it's interesting to note that the French still enjoy genuine smoked salmon; in fact there is a shop in Les Halles that sells nothing else (except for a wondrous range of dried mushrooms, and three kinds of caviare). Sometimes we are simply outbid for our own delicacies by people who care a bit more about what they are eating.

Anyhow, I don't mind the taste of smoked trout, and in order to make it something special, developed this recipe for our restaurant. When it meets the diner in this guise, the smoked fish is always moist, light and fluffy – something that it is hard to claim for the average trout embalmed in supermarket plastic.

This dish is much easier to make if you can lay your hands on proper 'leaf' gelatine, in those fragile, wafer-thin sheets. It is marvellous stuff and takes a lot of the responsibility for measuring accurately away from the harassed cook. It also seems so straightforward and easy to dissolve that you cannot help wondering why the gelatine manufacturers persist with those small envelopes of powder – perhaps like the mustard pioneers their real profits lie in what you waste rather than what you use.

The other partner in this dish is an Eastern one – coriander. You need the fresh green leaves which are available in small and pricey bunches from supermarkets, or large and cheap clumps from backstreet shops with an ethnic clientele; coriander seed, which plays a starring role in curry powder, is another thing altogether. Coriander leaves have the same kind of slightly hot taste you find in watercress, and a very distinctive flavour all of their own. The trout and coriander combine together brilliantly, with the coriander supplying the bite that horseradish provides in that other old favourite: smoked trout with creamed horseradish.

INTRODUCTION

This dish needs fresh green coriander, but over and above that, you may choose to experiment. Try it out with smoked mackerel, or even smoked salmon – but to my taste good smoked salmon shouldn't be expended on a dish like this, and cheap smoked salmon is too salty. Smoked mackerel mousse comes under the *perhaps* heading.

What is worth considering, is applying this recipe in a slightly lateral fashion to make a horseradish mousse, either to accompany cold roast beef, or fillets of good smoked trout. It's simple to make, and looks terrific if you set it in little moulds. Take a jar of shop-bought hot horseradish sauce (check the ingredients list for an early mention of the word horseradish and avoid those brands which include turnip), put it into a food processor with an equal quantity of double cream and a squeeze of lemon juice, add gelatine (first dissolved in a little water) at a rate of 2 sheets per half pint of ingredients. Whizz in the food processor until everything thickens up like whipped cream, pack into moulds, chill to set and serve. Very tasty.

INGREDIENTS

6 fillets of smoked trout (i.e. 3 whole fish).

25–50 g (1–1½ oz) fresh coriander leaves

The juice of a lime (or a lemon at a pinch).

A 284 ml carton of double cream.

2 leaves of gelatine.

Salt and freshly ground black pepper.

METHOD

Take six moulds: ramekins, dariole moulds, small glasses, egg cups – whatever your fancy. Obviously if you use very small moulds the mixture will go further but people will still eat the same amount so you'll have to serve an appropriate number to each diner; it's a question of swings and roundabouts. Set up the food processor (and I'm afraid that in this instance nothing else will do), add the trout fillets, the coriander, and the lime juice and whizz fiercely. When it's suitably mushy, add salt and freshly ground black pepper to taste. Soften your sheets of gelatine in water and then dissolve them in a minimum of water – either in the microwave or in a pan on top of the stove – run the food processor on 'slow' and add the dissolved gelatine and the cream until well mixed, then turn up the speed until the mixture becomes fluffy and thick. Imagine you were whipping cream. Then stop. Because if you overdo it your mousse will turn to butter. Transfer the mixture to the moulds and chill to set. Turning them out shouldn't be a problem, just run them briefly under a hot tap.

The finished mousses will give you a whole new slant on smoked fish.

Number Seven – Strawberry Dessert Wine

In which a lady writing to the Telegraph
shares her problems with us

This recipe was developed from one that appeared on the letters page of the *Daily Telegraph* some decades ago. The original was in the form of one of those wonderful letters, blithe and unconcerned – not a hint of wars, famines, pestilence, or troubles of any kind. I picture the writer as one of those indomitable persons whose tweed coat is belted with a dog lead and who wears unsuitable hats. Anyway I'm indebted to her for the germ of an idea that became this recipe.

Her letter went something like this: 'Dear Sir, In the summer we find the terrific glut of strawberries very trying, and this handy recipe is a good way of using them up . . . ' It went on to set out a recipe for a home-made wine which I couldn't make work. For one thing it relied upon the wild yeasts to be found upon the strawberries and they are notoriously unreliable, and for another it failed to address the problems of acidity which you are bound to get with a citrus fruit like strawberries. There was one other facet of the original recipe that leapt off the page. After a short fermentation, and whilst there was still a honey-sweet sugar concentration in the fledgling wine, she killed off the yeast and fortified the wine by adding a bottle of 'good malt whisky'! Now this I had to try.

If you can keep your hands off this wine for a year or two it becomes very fine indeed. Luscious, sweet as a *Trockenbeerenauslese*, and carrying off a high alcoholic content uncannily well. The acid of the strawberries is balanced by body and sweetness. However, this is a wine that carries with it the onus of responsibility. On one occasion my wife and I took a bottle to a dinner party; a dinner party that was going well enough for the host to run out of the rosé he was serving to two of the ladies as a pre-dinner drink. He saw our strawberry wine on the sideboard, it looked an appropriate colour and within minutes it was doing sterling service as a stand-in aperitif. If the party was going well before this high-octane top-up it went even better after it. The participants still talk in hushed tones about that evening and the husband of one of the ladies concerned subsequently asked me for another bottle – 'for their anniversary'.

The whiskey in this recipe cannot be tasted in the finished wine. When we were hoteliers we even put it forward in a blind tasting at which an eminent Master of Wine not only failed to spot the hidden whiskey, but also placed the wine's origins somewhere in the Loire Valley.

INTRODUCTION

If you are not an habitual home winemaker do not be put off by amateur winemakers' Fair Isle sweaters and socks-worn-with-sandals image. Wine-making is painstaking rather than difficult, and in many ways is very similar to feeding a newborn baby – the first and overriding rule is that every utensil should be kept absolutely sterile.

Take care over every stage and try and be patient, winemaking is like beekeeping, gardening or stockbreeding: you are husbanding a natural process and encouraging nature to do something for you. There are basic rules, mainly concerned with simple chemical reactions and keeping your fermenting wine fit and free from infections. What cannot be set down is a rigid timetable. Things may not happen as quickly or as slowly as you expect. You're working in a kitchen and not in a laboratory, you cannot control temperature, humidity, light levels, etc., for months on end. Even with three hundred years' practice and a great deal of money, famous French Chateaux occasionally produce a duff batch. (They solve this problem of inconsistency by calling all the years when everything goes to plan 'great' years and charging a hefty premium.)

EQUIPMENT

This section presumes that you're not even a dabbler at winemaking and outlines the basics – if you know better, ignore it and skip ahead. For this recipe, which aims to make about a gallon of wine, you'll need:

two 2-gallon buckets; a fine-mesh straining net; a bottle brush; a measuring jug; a syphon tube; two clear 1-gallon demijohns; a pierced bung that fits the demijohns and a fermentation lock to fit the bung; kitchen funnels and strainers; seven bottles and corks; some kind of corking device. All this lot can be found in your kitchen or in that dying breed, the homebrew shop. It is all relatively cheap; the whole lot shouldn't cost more than a decent leg of lamb! If you're a kitchen paraphernalia addict you can also get the deluxe-patented-latest versions of all the above and a whole lot more from the same shops, it's really up to you.

CHEMICALS AND INGREDIENTS
1 pack (100 g) sodium metabisulphite

1 small pack Campden tablets

1 small pack (50 g) vitamin C powder

1 pack (100 g) pectin-destroying enzyme

1 small pack vitamin B1 (thiamine) in tiny tablets

1 small pack yeast nutrient

1 small pack potassium sorbate

1 small bottle of tannin drops

2 oranges

1 sachet winemaker's yeast

2 kg (4 lb 8 oz) ripe strawberries

1 kg (2 lb 4 oz) ripe bananas

1.5 kilos (3 lb 5 oz) granulated sugar

1 bottle Irish whiskey

METHOD

Having assembled everything, embark upon your winemaking. But as mentioned earlier, do not expect to stick slavishly to the timetable. (If you are experienced at home winemaking much of this will err on the side of being a bit obvious, so feel free to skip ahead.)

DAY 1

Clean everything thoroughly with sterilising solution made up as follows: two litres of water, plus two teaspoons of sodium metabisulphite, plus one teaspoon of vitamin C powder. Don't breathe in the fumes of this liquid any more than is necessary.

Rinse well.

Peel your bananas and chop them into a saucepan. Just cover them with water and simmer them for twenty minutes or so until they are a grey sludge. Do not be put off by its unappetising appearance. Let it cool and then strain it through a very fine sieve or straining bag into one of your buckets. (Remember everything must be sterilised.) You'll have about half a pint of strange, thick, viscous, not exactly clear liquid. This was the invention of pioneer home winemakers and is called 'banana gravy'. It will be responsible for giving your finished wine its body.

Hull your strawberries and whizz them in a food processor, then add the strawberry sludge to the banana gravy in your sterilised bucket. Then crush one Campden tablet between two spoons and pop the powder in; this will see that any errant wild yeasts are killed off. Also stir in a teaspoon of pectin-destroying enzyme which will break down the pectin molecules into bite-sized bits and save your wine from developing a pectin haze at a later stage. Also add a few drops of tannin solution; tannin not only acts as a preservative, it also helps prevent hazes. As to exactly how much tannin to use, it is best to follow the directions on the particular brand you're using, but remember that we are aiming for a light pink wine and it will require less tannin than you'd need in red. Then top up your bucket with water until it contains around a gallon of liquid, this is the 'must'. Cover and leave overnight.

DAY 2

Make up a yeast starter bottle by squeezing the oranges into a saucepan, adding an ounce or so of sugar, and a good pinch of yeast nutrient. Warm it gently until it's at about blood heat, pop it into a small sterilised bottle and add your sachet of yeast, shake to mix, then plug the top with a wad of cotton wool and put it to one side in a warm place for two or three hours for the yeast to start fizzin' and frothin'. Any winemaking yeast seems to work pretty well but you may be reassured by buying 'Sauternes type' or one suggested for white wine. Stir into your bucket half the sugar, a teaspoon of yeast nutrient, two B1 tablets, and the starter bottle contents. Cover the bucket and leave it to ferment, somewhere that the temperature is stable. It doesn't have to be hot, just steady.

DAY 3
Stir the bucket and re-cover.

DAY 4
Stir the bucket and re-cover.

DAY 5
Stir the bucket and re-cover.

DAY 6
Stir the bucket and re-cover.

DAY 7
Stir in the other half of the sugar, and strain the contents through the fine straining bag into a demijohn and add another teaspoonful of yeast nutrient. A clear demijohn helps because you can see what's going on

inside, but the wine will lose colour if it is left in daylight, so from here on you should either put the demijohn in the dark (under the stairs or in the cellar), or make it a little lightproof jacket from a bin bag. Fit the bung with the fermentation lock and put water with a good pinch of sodium metabisulphite into the 'one-way-bend' of the airlock so that your concoction can bubble away without air or infection getting in. It will go on fermenting for some while, depending on: how warm it is; the strength of the yeast; how much sugar was in the strawberries; and a host of other variables. If you're an expert with a hydrometer, aim for a final specific gravity of about 1005; if not, you could do worse than taste the young wine occasionally and decide for yourself when the sweetness has diminished enough. Be careful to maintain your hygiene standards and keep infection away from the wine throughout this procedure.

So six or seven weeks later . . .

Syphon the wine into your second demijohn leaving the sediment behind. Make the volume up with water so that the level is at the shoulders of the bottle. Add 1 teaspoonful of potassium sorbate which will kill off the yeast and leave the wine fixed at that particular level of sweetness.

After another three weeks . . .

Syphon it again, leaving the sediment behind, and make up the volume as before.

Go on with this procedure until you have a clear rosé wine. Twice should do it. When you have a clear rosé wine, bottling time has arrived. Sterilise your seven bottles, and then line them up and divide the Irish whiskey equally between them. I prefer Irish whiskey because it is softer tasting, and cheaper. Even the cheapest Irish whiskey is malt whiskey, which is a fact you don't often hear bandied about by Scotsmen. Then use the syphon to fill up each bottle with wine. The contents should come up to within half an inch of the bottom of the cork. If it looks as if you are going to fall short of the seven bottles, share it out carefully and make up the volume with some water. Then insert the corks which you have previously soaked in sterilising solution. Label. Hide. And wait.

This wine will be good after eighteen months, better after two years, then three and then so forth. The oldest I have is some ten years old and it's glorious. Sweet, but not cloying – and still defying anyone to recognise its secret Irish ingredient.

Number Eight – Cup-of-Tea Cake

In which we confess a debt to Mary Day and a
Mrs Asquith of Harrogate

When asked to name a crucial date in the history of gastronomy, 1934 doesn't immediately spring to mind, although perhaps it should, because that year saw the first publication of *Farmers Weekly*. It also saw the first editor of the 'Home Section', Mary Day, begin to marshal the influx of recipes which readers sent in from all over the country. Within a year there was enough material for a book – *Farmhouse Fare*. And over the years to come that book went through an arduous succession of reprints and revisions.

Over the years I have always kept a lookout for this book at car-boot sales and in second-hand bookshops. In the beginning my aim was to find a replacement for my mother's old, tatty and cherished copy which had gone missing never to be seen again, but then I needed another copy for my daughter, and one for my son, and as gifts – so I am always in the market for copies of the 1974 edition.

It's a wonderful book, and during its first forty years sold over half a million copies. One of its most attractive features is the practical nature of the recipes it sets out – and despite referring to itself as 'this little book' it carries nearly one thousand with over fifty in the section on pig curing and by-products alone.

So for nettle syrup, Suffolk new-milk cheese, scruggin cake, furniture cream or turnip brose you need look no further. All the recipes are written by people who know what they're doing, and they expect you to know what you're doing too. Instructions like 'put it in front of the fire until nicely browned', or 'stir the pig's blood by hand whilst it is still warm to remove the veins (which will adhere to the fingers and be easily removed)' are not run of the mill in the age of the microwave. I can always find the page with the cup-of-tea cake recipe on it because a succession of cake-mixture spills and splashes have determined that this is where my copy falls open on its own.

Basically, the recipe submitted by Mrs Asquith of Harrowgate (and yes, that is how they spell it, at least in this instance) is for a boiled fruit cake. In the days when you used to sieve dried fruit to remove any small stones; when the fruit was much drier; when it was not lightly coated in mineral oil to keep it separate; then a boiled fruit cake was one of the ways you could make sure that your cake was succulent to the last slice and that the fruit didn't pull all the fluid out of the mixture during cooking. You simply boiled the fruit in liquid until it had absorbed enough and then let it go cold before proceeding. Nowadays dried fruit is much less dried than it used to be, but this technique will ensure that you end up with a particularly moist cake. I have also changed Mrs Asquith's recipe by doubling the amount of spice, adding another egg, and increasing the amount of, and kinds of, dried fruit. One of the idiosyncrasies of *Farmhouse Fare* as a cookbook, which was retained by the revising editor of the 1974 edition, was a slight tendency towards thrift (cakes contain a lot of flour and not too many eggs; there are plenty of nourishing, economical recipes like pilchard hotpot and savoury sheep's head), so my recipe would probably have been classed as unduly extravagant.

INTRODUCTION

I offer two different method paragraphs for this recipe. One follows Mrs Asquith's original; and the other makes use of one of those new-fangled food-processor contrivances. I would also recommend that you line your cake tin with a circle of baking parchment for the bottom and a strip around the sides like a chimney. Silicone baking paper is so miraculously efficient that you cannot help wondering whether this alleged spin-off from the avionics industry might not have been the real reason for the entire space race.

As the recipe calls for a 'cup of tea' I have had to make one or two assumptions. First that we are talking about tea with milk in it and secondly about how big the cup should be. I have also tried out a few different kinds of tea. I would like to be able to relate that the delicate flavour of Earl Grey makes a great difference, but the truth is that it doesn't – any good strong-drinking, tea-bag tea seems fine.

This cake keeps well in a sealed plastic box but like 90 percent of all home baking, tastes best warm and about two hours out of the oven.

INGREDIENTS

175 g (6 oz) unsalted butter

400 g (14 oz) mixed fruit – choose for yourself from sultanas, raisins, apricots, dates, glacé cherries, candied peel

250 ml (9 fl oz) strong tea with milk

350 g (12 oz) self-raising flour

175 g (6 oz) caster sugar

2 level tsp bicarbonate of soda

3 heaped tsp mixed spice

2 free-range eggs (size 1)

METHOD – MRS ASQUITH'S

'Melt butter in pan, add fruit and tea. Bring to boil and simmer for two minutes. Cool. Sieve dry ingredients, add boiled mixture and eggs, mix well. Bake.'

METHOD – ALTERNATIVE

My favourite tin for this cake is round with a removable base (21 cm or

8 in in diameter and 8 cm or 3 in deep). Line it with a circle of silicone baking parchment for the base and around the sides. The silicone paper should stand proud of the top of the cake tin by about 7 cm (2½ in), and it will help avoid burning on the top of the cake. Pre-heat your oven to gas mark 4 / 350°F / 180°C.

Melt the butter in the pan, and add the fruit and tea. Bring it to the boil and simmer for two minutes, turn off the heat and stand the whole pan in cold water for ten minutes. The fruit and tea mixture doesn't have to be absolutely cold, but you don't want it so hot that it starts the cooking process. Put the flour, sugar, spice and bicarbonate into your food processor and whizz until well mixed. Beat the two eggs with a fork, then strain the liquid from the saucepan into the eggs and add it all to the processor bowl.

Whizz some more until you have a smooth well-mixed cake batter. Then add the fruit and any remaining dregs from the saucepan, whizz very briefly, long enough to distribute the fruit evenly, but not so long that you chop it to pulp. Pour the whole lot into the lined cake tin. Bake. The cake should take between an hour and a half, and an hour and three quarters, so have a look at it after about an hour. The old-fashioned test of 'check with a skewer and the cake is done when it comes out dry' really does work. Take the cake from the tin and let it cool, still in its baking parchment liner, on a rack. This is a really delicious cake, so when you try it, raise a teacup to Mrs Asquith and all those other farmers' wives.

Number Nine – Mash to Die For

In which we are able to confirm that Messrs
Gault and Millau know a thing or two

You know how it is, you read about a restaurant, a very famous restaurant where there is a year-long waiting list for a table; where the bill will be enormous; where the food is ambrosia . . . and you find yourself planning a visit. Fredy Giradet's little place in Crissier was such a restaurant, and all my dreams and hopes remain intact as I never made my pilgrimage and now the restaurant is no more. Giradet was self-evidently a major star in the chefs' firmament. But for me he was the man who made mash famous.

All the guide books praised his deft touch; Gault Millau gave him the Clé d'Or; and all the while one of his signature dishes was mashed potato. At about this time Paul Bocuse was at the Elysée Palace whipping up 'Soupe aux truffes Elysée' as a thank you when Valéry Giscard d'Estaing awarded him the Legion d'honneur for his services to French cuisine. Imagine it, a truffle soup hidden under a light puff pastry dome; if that's the sort of grandstand stuff that gets you medals, what did Fredy deserve for redefining mashed potato?

My research into this wonder spud led me to Fredy Giradet's book, *Cuisine Spontanée*. Already things were not quite what they seem. How can you title a book 'Spontaneous Cooking' and then include a dish like 'Beatilles de lapin aux morilles et truffes noires' – a simple little number, some of whose ingredients are rabbit livers; rabbit kidneys; morels; truffles; shallots; new-season onion; Madeira; white port; and truffle juice? All in all, the kind of things we all have lying around the store cupboard just waiting for some chance visitor to give us an opportunity to show off our spontaneous cooking skills.

Undaunted, I read on. His principles are very good. Good food starts with good ingredients and taking care. I agree entirely, and it is no surprise that I relish his mashed potato (the selfsame one that is supposed to have made the guide inspector swoon). Fred's mash was made from new potatoes with olive oil and cream. And for me the olive oil was the key to this recipe. Obviously just how your purée of potatoes turns out will always depend on what potatoes you start with – the amount of starch in the raw potato will be the governing factor in the final texture. So my first point of disagreement was with the choice of new potatoes. Old potatoes are generally more floury and make better mash, as they absorb more of the nice things you put into them.

I'm afraid I couldn't face pushing spuds through a sieve or Mouli-légumes – once again I cling to a food processor, despite the lurking danger that overuse can make the mash gluey. So my 'mash to die for' owes much, if not all, to Monsieur Giradet. Now the problem lies more in finding a sausage that is worthy of accompanying it.

INTRODUCTION

This recipe uses olive oil as a flavouring, so the olive oil you choose should be the most flavourful you can lay your hands on; that seriously expensive extra virgin, or that dark green stuff in an odd bottle that you brought back from Tuscany – either would be perfect. But the oil is the flavouring, so first of all taste a teaspoonful and see if you like it. If you do, all well and good.

And of course with the proliferation of other tasty oils on the supermarket shelves – sesame, argan, grapeseed, hazelnut, pumpkin-seed, walnut, pistachio – so there's plenty of scope for informed experiment.

When we had the hotel and restaurant I used to serve this mash, and as a consequence I had to endure a period of sustained hatred from the waitresses. I used to make the purée and then put it into a flat oven-proof dish, sprinkle cheese and breadcrumbs on the top and pop it into the oven to crisp over. This combination of juggling with a nearly red hot dish, and a spoon-bendingly hard crust led to bad feeling from the silver service brigade. But the result was jolly tasty all the same.

INGREDIENTS

These are the right proportions, please adjust precise quantities to suit.

1 kg (2 lb 4 oz) main crop potatoes

100 ml (3½ fl oz) double cream

100 ml (3½ fl oz) good olive oil

½ a bunch spring onions

Salt and freshly ground black pepper

METHOD

Peel your potatoes and boil them in salted water until they are well cooked – just before they fall away to mush. Strain and leave them in the colander to steam for a minute or two. Chop up the spring onions, using the both the white bits and the light-green bits.

Put the potatoes into the food processor. Whizz them fast. Add the cream and whizz some more. Rest the mixture a minute. Add the oil and whizz some more. Add the spring onions and whizz a little to mix. I like that silky, starchy texture. Adjust seasoning with salt and freshly ground black pepper. Serve immediately or put in a fireproof dish in the oven under a layer of grated hard cheese and some plain breadcrumbs to keep hot and form a crispy top.

Number Ten – Beer-Cured Ham

In which a good friend takes to his bed
in mid-afternoon

This recipe first saw the light of day when we were living in a cottage in Devon and had some friends to stay for Christmas. It all took place some time ago in those fondly remembered years – 'BC' – that is to say before children. We had a wonderful Christmas Day, a lie-in preceded Buck's Fizz, a little light unwrapping and then lunch at about three, followed by a nap and a good deal to drink and some of those excellent turkey sandwiches with stuffing and bread sauce in them.

Boxing Day was Johnny's undoing. We had put together a cold table and the star turn was a small beer-cured ham. To say that it proved popular would be a peculiarly English understatement. At this point I must give Johnny his due: for a relatively small man he ate a prodigious amount of cold ham. Afterwards this surfeit obliged him to retire to his bed for a lie down which lasted until lunchtime the following day. All I would proffer by way of comment is to suggest that you try this recipe for yourself and that when faced with a delicious and succulent plate of home-cured ham you strive to observe one of my godmother's favourite maxims: 'You should always leave the table,' she would say, 'feeling that you could eat just a little bit more.'

Once upon a time, not so very long ago, every farmer's wife would know the ins and outs and whys and wherefores of pickling, salting, curing, and all manner of pre-freezer ways of keeping meat past slaughter day. Today, factories around Britain pay lip service to these secrets while they put pork into huge machines like cold tumble dryers to tenderise it, then inject it with salt water from a battery of needles, and double-check that there is enough saltpetre to make even the dullest pig leg blush ham pink.

Did you know that the Danish landrace pig has been selectively bred over the last few decades so that it now has an extra vertebra? This extra bone means it has a longer back and that there is now a more profitable ratio of bacon to killing weight than in other unadapted pigs. With these kinds of priorities, it is no wonder that they taste like they do.

Try this recipe for a home-pickled ham. Then compare the flavour, texture and price with the finest reconstituted pinkly gleaming ham that the supermarket can offer. It'll be no contest, and for something that sounds tricky this recipe is a remarkably simple procedure – as it had to be when housewives used to fit it into their busy schedule with all the other day-to-day chores.

Later on, when you're enjoying the fruits of your labours, you'll have to be careful. The two things you'll have to guard against are overeating, and excessive boasting about your own beer-cured ham.

INTRODUCTION

In times gone by, most large kitchens would have had a pickling crock, capable of taking a couple of whole hams. If they have one at all nowadays it tends to be smaller, full of dried flowers and standing in pride of place on the top of a hand-distressed, limed-oak kitchen unit.

The amateur winemaking fraternity, however, can help. Simply visit your local homebrew shop and you'll find a cheap five-gallon bucket with a tightly fitting lid, designed for fermenting wine and beer. This is just the job for pickling your Christmas ham. Failing that, pick out a small dustbin, providing it has a good lid.

When you buy your leg of pork to try this recipe, it will probably cross your mind that commercial hams cost a great deal more than legs of pork. You may also wonder why. Curing a ham is a caring, labour-intensive task that doesn't fit in with the time-and-motion attitudes of modern factories. Producers respond the only way they know how by putting the price up. So carefully choose the leg of pork you are going to pickle; shortly it will emerge transformed into a much more valuable ham, so you might as well start with a decent leg of pork. If you read recipes written before the war, much mention is made of 'to cure a pig of between twenty-five and thirty stones' and 'take a leg of pork weighing over twenty-five lb'. Times have changed and so have pigs: modern recipes talk of legs of pork weighing approximately 6 kg (13 lb). I would recommend a middle course: explain to your butcher what you are going to do and ask for a fresh (not frozen) leg of pork, well fatted and weighing between 6.5 kg and 7.5 kg (13 lb and 16½ lb).

INGREDIENTS

1 leg of pork, fresh; well fatted; weighing between 6.5 kg
   and 7.5 kg (13 lb and 16½ lb)
450 g (1 lb) black treacle
700 g (1 lb 10 oz) cooking salt
125 g (4½ oz) muscovado sugar
12 g (½ oz) black peppercorns
25 g (1 oz) pounded mace
3 litres tinned Guinness
3 litres water

METHOD FOR THE CURING

I am presuming that you want to enjoy this dish on Boxing Day, when it will offer a welcome respite to a family faced with going 'cold turkey'. So this schedule stems from that assumption.

Start in the third or fourth week of November. Take your leg of pork and make sure that the knuckle bone protrudes from the trotter end. If not, cut away the meat so that there's an 8 cm (3 in) shank sticking out. Give it a good wash and pat it dry with some kitchen towel. Put it on a large dish or a plastic tray. Take the muscovado sugar and 200 g (7 oz) of the salt and rub it into the meat, being particularly careful to rub the shank well so that the salt can run along the bone and into the meat. Cover the joint with a bit of foil and put it in a cool place overnight.

The next day gather up the sklutchy mess with your hands and rub it into the pork.

Repeat this process again after another twelve hours.

Then make sure that your five-gallon fermenting bucket (or the equivalent) is scrupulously clean. Put all the other pickle ingredients into your largest saucepan and bring them to the boil. Allow it all to cool. Then you have to submerge your leg of pork in the pickle until Christmas. The best way to do this is to wedge the pork down under the liquid with a heavy china plate, or glass casserole lid, or something similar. The guiding principles are these: first try and arrange the pork so that the majority of it is in contact with the liquid (i.e. don't press the cut side against the plastic of the bucket), and secondly do ensure that it is completely submerged: the salty marinade is what preserves the meat. Pop the lid on and put it away until Christmas.

METHOD FOR COOKING

On Christmas Eve open the bucket. Do not be put off by the smell –
rather like an old brewery on pipe-cleaning day. Do not be put off by the
looks – once we opened our bucket to reveal a skin of virulent mould
which had grown across the top of the liquid, but under the surface all
was well and the end product was delicious as expected.

Take out the blackened, wrinkled ham. Fill your largest pot with water,
pop the ham in and put it on to cook. Then you can hunt around for an
outside drain to pour away the foul-smelling black liquid!

Bring your ham to the boil and then simmer. Work out the cooking
time from the original weight of the leg of pork and allow forty-five
minutes per kg (twenty minutes per pound). After two hours cooking
take the ham out and skin it – garden birds dote on this skin. Then
return the ham until cooking is completed. When it is finished remove it
from the pan and let it cool, and before it is completely cold score the
fat, and dust with breadcrumbs in the old-fashioned way. Pop it in the
fridge to carve on Boxing Day. A ham cured this way won't look pink
and shiny because there's no saltpetre in the cure, so it's more likely to
look grey. But it will smell pleasantly gamey, and taste out of this world.
Just try not to overeat . . .

Number Eleven – Honey and Ginger Ice Cream

In which we ginger up an old favourite

Everyone loves ice cream. But from that moment when the first cone slips out of your two-year-old hand on a one-way trip to the pavement, ice cream can all too often mean disappointment – lots of it. One of my first, and probably my most exciting, encounters with ice cream occurred when my best friend James Dawes emptied the contents of his tub over the balcony of the Regal Cinema in Leamington Spa. It fell on to the head of an unfortunate elderly gentleman seated in the stalls below, whose scream of anguished surprise was enough to ensure that not only was the show interrupted, but that the lights were turned on as well. Only a hurried visit to the gents saved James and me from a fate worse than death, and even then we missed the main film. After such adventures, ice cream has a lot to live up to.

However you dress it up, ice cream remains frozen custard. And the unstoppable rise of those natty red, blue and yellow tins of Messrs Bird mean that custard-making is a dying art. Little wonder good ice cream is so hard to find.

Ice cream also gets top billing as a villain in the cholesterol war. And on top of that it could be laden with dangerously undercooked egg yolks. At this point I should like to stress that if you are queasy about egg yolks don't use this recipe, although the method ensures that the eggs will get hotter than the magic 72°C required for safety.

To make a truly wonderful ice cream, like the ice cream misty-eyed old-timers remember from before the war, you start with a truly wonderful custard. Plenty of egg yolks, real double cream. To make my honey and ginger ice cream you take that wonderful custard and replace some of the sugar with honey, then ginger everything up with some ginger. And don't be feeble about it, ginger should be hot. The joy of this dish comes from its hot taste and its cold velvety texture.

INTRODUCTION

Every book you read says that you can make superb ice cream in an ordinary refrigerator by freezing your mixture in a tray and stirring it from time to time. Perhaps I'm unique, but I can assure you that it doesn't work for me. On the other hand, an ice cream machine does. I've got a terrific one and if you don't own one yet I can only offer my sympathy. A good ice cream machine makes ice cream simple and that makes the investment worthwhile. Try and borrow one from a friend for a week or so and see for yourself. Obviously they all run at slightly different temperatures: there are those with detachable drums that you leave in the freezer to get cold and then replace on the machine; there are antique ones where you turn a handle and use salt and ice as your freezing agent; and there are state of the art machines that have their own freezer unit and are free-standing. This recipe tells you about the contents; how long you freeze and beat it for will depend on the exact way you want your ice cream. If you have an ice cream machine, hard-won experience, plus a little trial and error, will teach you how long and how cold you must churn for the perfect result.

I have already touched on the importance of buying your eggs carefully. As well as very fresh, wholesome eggs, you need to buy your cream wisely. Look out for farm-gate shops; we have one that sells Jersey cream altogether richer and more delicious than supermarket cream. For honey the same rules apply: small producers make nicer honey. And for ginger be sure to get crystallised ginger, sometimes known as 'cake ginger'. At a pinch, stem ginger will do but it's usually too wet and sloppy, and you should avoid the stem ginger from Chinese supermarkets which they rather puzzlingly stain red for good luck.

INGREDIENTS

The yolks of ten large fresh eggs
600 ml (1 pt) double cream
425 ml (15 fl oz) whole milk
100 g (3½ oz) caster sugar

175 g (6 oz) runny honey

350 g (12 oz) crystallised cake ginger

METHOD

Put the milk, cream and honey into a heavy saucepan and heat up on the stove. Heat it all slowly and do not let it boil. Beat the egg yolks with the sugar (an old-fashioned balloon whisk is ideal for this job); the posh books say you should beat until the ribbon stage but I find that hard to be exact about – thick and frothy would be my best suggestion. Then you have to mix your nearly boiling milk and cream and your room-temperature eggs. Your objective is gradually to increase the amount of heat in the combined mixture until the egg yolks start to cook and form a beautifully smooth emulsion with everything else. If you go too fast the eggs will curdle and all will be wasted. Some people recommend doing all this in a double saucepan because then it cannot ever boil, but it does take a long time. I prefer a low heat and whisking the liquid continually so that no one part of it gets more heat than the rest.

So to return to the nearly boiling milk and room-temperature frothy eggs. Pour half the nearly boiling liquid on to the eggs, beating as you do so. Beat thoroughly. Then pour the contents of that pan back on to the remaining milk in the heavy pan and carry on beating. Now you should have everything mixed together and hopefully uncurdled, carry on beating. Turn the heat up a fraction at a time, whilst continuing to stir and distribute that heat throughout the mixture. The liquid will thicken. Other books say that the custard is ready when it 'coats the back of a wooden spoon' – one more bit of terminology I find it hard to be sure about. The keynote is patience and increasing the heat cautiously. If it looks like you have a curdle imminent, lift the pan away and beat as if your custard depended on it, which it does. The best guide I can offer is to say that if the stuff in your pan looks like custard to you, then it is ready. Put it to one side.

Then get your ginger ready. I recommend popping two thirds of it into a food processor and whizzing it until it is finely chopped, scrape the 'almost-paste' that results into the custard, stir and leave it to cool. Take the other third of the ginger and chop it into tiny chunks by hand; this ginger should be in appreciably larger pieces than the rest.

Churn the ginger custard in your ice cream machine, and as it is starting to set add the larger ginger pieces. I cannot say how long it will take or whether you will need to do one batch or two, but I can say that most ice creams are served slightly too hard for my liking and that taking yours out of the deep freeze and into the fridge for an hour before serving will really help. I would also like to re-emphasise that this is essentially a fresh food and that it won't improve with keeping.

Once you have tasted this honey and ginger ice cream it will be well nigh impossible to enjoy commercial ice creams ever again – for all the temptations of their fake Italian names.

Number Twelve – Blackberry Duck

In which we discuss the proximity of ducks
to the briar patch

It was quite a shock when the head carpenter wandered his way through our still-unfinished hotel in Buxton and said, 'There are some ducks to see you at the back door.' We went to investigate and there they were, a duck and a drake mallard shouting for something to eat. They were extremely tame and very vocal in their demands for food. One of the electricians was most impressed and he volunteered to build a little ramp into the oven. 'Then,' he said, 'we could feed them a few oranges and walk them straight in for forty minutes at gas mark six.'

They came back regularly, and when on their last visit Mrs Duck brought a brood of fluffy baby ducks for inspection, my insensitive remarks about *en brochette* were not well received by the assembled waitresses.

Despite knowing these ducks personally we did put blackberry duck on to the menu, and it was a runaway success. Most of the credit must go to the ducks. At some expense we brought in Gressingham ducks, and very tasty they are too. It is said that these ducks are a cross between an Aylesbury and a wild mallard. The result is a wonderful duck to eat; it's not as fatty as the Aylesbury; it's meatier than a mallard; and it's not so big as a Barbary. It really is a bespoke duck, excellent in every respect.

If you can't lay your hands on a Gressingham, see if you cannot get your ducks from a small independent supplier or a good traditional butcher. There are pockets of excellence to be found all over the country. It is just a matter of hunting them out.

But to revert to this dish. I suppose the recipe came about through my dislike of Kir – a white wine and *crème de cassis* – and my preference for the trendy variant Mir – white wine with *crème de mure*. In a nutshell I never truly warmed to Ribena but was always partial to blackberries. So instead of sousing duck in blackcurrants as seemed to be the vogue, I decided to complement it with blackberries. After all, I reasoned, you are much more likely to come upon a duck in a briar patch than amongst the blackcurrant bushes.

Blackberry duck presents duck simply cooked and with a sauce that is the perfect foil to richness of the meat. And you can always use up the rest of the bottle of *crème de mure* by diluting it in the glass with plenty of champagne – delicious!

INTRODUCTION

Obviously shopping wisely plays an important part in getting this recipe exactly right. You need a magret de canard for each diner – that is to say one side of a whole duck breast with the skin. Obviously you will have access to different suppliers depending on where you live and how adventurous you are. I can vouch for Gressingham ducks; as for supermarket ducks, some are better than others. The duck breasts imported from France can be fabulous, providing they're not too big or too fatty – some seem to have been removed by chainsaw from a Barbary duck large enough to be called 'Sir' when met on a dark night.

These would be my guidelines: each magret should weigh about 275 grams (9½ oz); the meat should be dark red and not too coarse in texture; the fat should not be more than 7.5 mm (⅓ in) deep.

Over and above that, where to find the perfect duck is your affair. You'll also need a bottle of *crème de mure*, but that will present less of a problem, a good wine merchant or supermarket wine department with aspirations should prove helpful.

INGREDIENTS

1 magret de canard per person. (Sauce quantities for four.)
Salt and freshly ground black pepper
125 g (4½ oz) unsalted butter
110 g (4 oz) onions

75 ml (3 fl oz) *crème de mure*

50 ml (2 fl oz) red-wine vinegar

METHOD

Pre-heat your oven to max! Then get your duck breasts out of the fridge, salt them lightly and give them a couple of turns of freshly ground black pepper, then put them in a warm place so that they're not clammy-cold when you start to cook them.

When you're ready to start, put a little of the butter in a large frying pan and sear the duck breasts on both sides. Transfer the duck pieces to a roasting dish for the oven. If you can put them on a raised grill so that they are clear of the bottom of the dish all the better, and save the pan. The duck needs to cook in a very hot oven (near the top at gas mark 8 / 450°F / 230°C) for ten minutes. This will mean that the magrets come out pink and juicy. If you find them too pink for your taste give them an extra five minutes next time. They need to rest for five minutes after they come out of the oven before carving. During this cooking and resting time you can make the blackberry sauce.

If there is a large amount of duck fat in the pan you used earlier to sear the duck, pour some off but leave enough to get that ducky flavour. Add all but 25 grams (1 oz) of the remaining butter, melt it and add the onions chopped as finely as you can (the size of matchsticks cut across every 3 mm [⅛ in]). Slowly cook the onions until they're transparent and soft. Add the vinegar, turn up the heat, and stir as it boils away to almost nothing. Then add the *crème de mure* and cook briefly to get rid of the alcohol. Then add the butter you've kept back, a little at a time, and whisk as you do so. Season with salt and pepper to taste. You'll have a velvety, dark, rich sauce. Carve the duck breasts across into slices and arrange these simply on top of a pool of sauce on each plate. Serve immediately.

Number Thirteen – Brandy Butter

In which we can confirm that you
heard it first on The Grapevine

I never paid much attention to brandy butter, which is rather surprising as I was brought up in a family that tended towards *dry* food. With the exception of a few classic sauces we ate our meat with its own juices; our strawberries with clotted rather than runny cream; and bread and butter pudding *au naturel*. Christmas pudding was always served with 'hard sauce' and not custard.

So perhaps I was subconsciously groomed to favour brandy butter from an early age. However, it would take a strange diner to deny that the cold, rich, almost crisp taste of well-made brandy butter doesn't make a perfect foil for a blazing slice of soggy Christmas pudding.

But as I mentioned, I never gave it much heed until the late Peter Pugson rang up during the first November we had the hotel in Buxton. Every year, in the run-up to Christmas, Peter of the eponymous and all-encompassing cheese shop printed a special issue of his regular news-letter – *The Grapevine* – which, as well as trying to concentrate everyone's mind on Stilton in good time, so that the cheese can be brought to a peak of ripeness for Christmas Day, dealt with anything and everything to do with the festive board. What, he wanted to know, was to be 'the Campion literary contribution'? How we came to decide that the Peak District was crying out for a treatise on brandy butter I do not know, but that is what I wrote about. So it was for *The Grapevine* that this recipe was originally honed to perfection. Making brandy butter is not as straightforward as it first appears. If you dive into that great stand-by Mrs Beeton's *All About Cookery*, you'll find that her recipe for 'hard sauce', as she calls it, contains optional ground almonds, optional egg whites, and between a teaspoonful and a tablespoonful of brandy. (Obviously the precise amount of spirit varies depending on whether you are entertaining a Methodist minister or the local squire.) Mrs B's recipe also falls into the number-one trap for would-be brandy-butter creators – icing sugar. Personally I believe that icing sugar alone doesn't give the brandy butter the requisite *bite*: that tiniest crunch which so improves each forkful of rich, moist pudding.

The recipe that follows is the one I developed for *The Grapevine* Christmas issue, and which gained us a bushel of compliments when we served brandy butter in the hotel.

INTRODUCTION

When you've tried this recipe for brandy butter I hope that you will be emboldened and rifle the drinks cabinet to make Armagnac butter; or

Marc de Bourgogne butter; or Cointreau butter (although if attempting Cointreau butter, you would be advised to leave out the fruit juice which should be included in the other recipes).

As is often the case, the quality of whatever you're making can only ever reflect the quality of the ingredients you use, so I'm afraid that if you use rough 'grape brandy', you'll end up with rough 'grape brandy butter'. On the other hand when you choose a delicate, after-dinner, sipping brandy and a nice unsalted premium butter you'll end up with a brandy butter that's truly a delight.

INGREDIENTS

100 g (3½ oz) unsalted butter
150 g (5½ oz) icing sugar
100 g (3½ oz) caster sugar
50 ml (2 fl oz) best brandy
A squeeze of fresh orange juice

METHOD

The important thing is to get air into the finished product, so cream the butter well with the icing sugar, working it in a little at a time. Then add the fruit juice (which I have included to prevent the brandy butter being too sickly) and the brandy, again a little at a time. Then finally add the caster sugar whilst continuing to work the mixture. Keep your brandy butter in the fridge until good and cold, then enjoy it melting over a self-indulgent portion of Christmas pudding. But don't keep brandy butter for more than a couple of days even in the fridge – there's no substitute for fresh!

Number Fourteen – North Country Plum Pudding

In which we spend some time delving into a
musty tea chest near Hornsea, East Riding

My wife's grandmother lived just outside Hornsea in a pretty farmhouse on a hill. As the bitter wind sweeps in across the North Sea from Scandinavia, this is where it shakes its coat and wipes its feet! When she died, well into her eighties, the old lady was living alone in much the same style as she had always done. She was on the electric but preferred to cook on the range; there was a cold water tap and an outside toilet; there was even a bath, but since new it had only seen service as a repository for newspapers. There was also a larder full of old and complex patent cream separators, Horlicks whisks, defunct preserving jars and fifty years of kitchen history.

In an old tea chest there were also a good many cookery books. At this point the tale starts to veer away from the romantic ideal. How much nicer it would have been if the recipe book we found had been a genuine sixteenth-century vellum original. Instead it was a nice little book published by Foulsham in their Home Library series (I don't know exactly when as there's no date in it anywhere but it looks as if it was just before, or just after, the Second World War – the cover price is seven shillings and sixpence). The book is called *Peggy Hutchinson's Old English Cookery Book*, and it's got one or two really cracking recipes in it. This is one of them.

This recipe is for an authentic North Country plum pudding and what makes it so unusual is all the things it leaves out. Picture a plum pudding like the ones that used to be illustrated in the *Beano* and nineteenth-century *Punch* cartoons – round, brownish and speckled with large juicy raisins. Well that's exactly what you end up with when you follow this recipe.

If you'd been asked to create such a pudding your thoughts would probably have turned towards sponge puddings. Eggs would play a part, perhaps butter, and self-raising flour or baking powder; all the dry ingredients would need the eggs to bind them together, or some milk, or some water.

This pudding is remarkable for what it omits. No eggs, no baking powder, no liquid of any kind. The leading players in this drama are carrot and potato. Mrs Hutchinson says in her book that this recipe was used by the cottagers of Bishopston – wherever that is – and that at the time of writing – whenever that was – it was already one hundred and fifty years old. As you read the ingredients list you realise that being poor two centuries ago was a more serious business than it is now. Today all the ingredients for this pudding to feed six will cost less than a single Danish pastry.

And there is one further amazing revelation that will come from trying out this recipe. Against all sceptical expectations, it is absolutely delicious. Time and time again I have asked diners to name the ingredients after a blind tasting, and so far no one has ever got them right. It turns out surprisingly light, a good colour, pleasantly spiced and full of succulent fruit. It's glorious.

INTRODUCTION

The folk of Bishopston had one thing in plenty – time. This pudding has to be mixed up and then left to stand for two days before cooking. It works on a very clever principle – the dry ingredients, like the fruit, draw the moisture out of the wet ingredients, like the raw carrot and the potato, so that the fruit plumps up. As this is happening the flavour of the spices and sugar is spreading throughout the mixture. When the pudding comes to the table you would never guess that it had a carrot or potato in it. You can either make this as a single large pudding in a traditional pudding basin or you can pack the mixture into small dariole moulds (about 6 cm high and 4 cm wide at the mouth – 2½ in by 1½ in). Personally I like to serve individual puddings each sitting on top of its own pool of custard. When we had the restaurant, our waitresses and kitchen staff always referred to these little puddings as 'hand grenades'.

INGREDIENTS

100 g (3½ oz) grated raw carrot

100 g (3½ oz) cooked mashed potato

100 g (3½ oz) plain flour

100 g (3½ oz) shredded suet

100 g (3½ oz) raisins

100 g (3½ oz) currants

100 g (3½ oz) brown sugar

50 g (1½ oz) peel grated from several unwaxed lemons

1 heaped tsp mixed spice

METHOD

Combine together all the ingredients thoroughly with your hands and knead the mixture in a mixing bowl until it's like a stiff dough. Then put the bowl in the fridge for two days with a bit of clingfilm over it. If this resting time stretches to three or four days it doesn't seem to do the pudding any harm. When you're going to cook the pudding, mix up the mixture thoroughly – you'll be surprised by how the consistency has changed and then tamp it down into a pudding bowl well greased with butter, and cover the top with silicone baking parchment tied around the bowl lip. Follow the same procedure if you're filling individual dariole moulds. There should be mixture enough for six, and each should have its own little baking-paper cover.

Then steam away. The big pudding will take four hours, and the individual ones two hours. I find that these little steamed puddings heat up particularly well in the microwave, perhaps due to their moistness and uniformity, so I tend to get the steaming over with in advance, then keep them in the fridge until wanted and heat them through when serving. Be careful that microwaving doesn't leave you with a pudding that's like Vesuvius – red-hot at the centre and progressively chillier towards the surface. The individual ones heat up quite quickly and either kind should stand for a minute or two after heating and before serving. Doing it this way means that you can give your best attention to preparing the custard.

I can guarantee that this North Country plum pudding will surprise and delight anyone who loves classic puddings. It's just the thing to keep the north-east wind at bay.

Number Fifteen – Fools Rush In

In which we consider the adage,
'If you want to find a fool in the country, you'll
have to take one with you'

Pretty soon fool-making will be a lost art, and small children will have to be taken to folk museums if they are to enjoy a genuine fool. Admittedly 'Old Mother Hubbard's Range of Genuine Country Fool-Type Desserts' will have gained a thrusting 47.8 per cent market share, and her tasteful little plastic pots in the shape of miniature wickerwork milk churns will beckon seductively from every supermarket shelf. These little pots will be emblazoned with an ingredients panel listing such traditional rustic delights as xanthan gum, guar gum, stabiliser, E this and E that.

But the only people who can reasonably lay claim to the sobriquet fool are the purchasers of such impostors. How is it that something so simple, so refreshing, so rich, so economical and so delicious should be such a well-kept secret? Mrs Beeton doesn't list fool, Delia Smith's *Cookery Course* doesn't mention it, in fact you are hard put to find any reference to it anywhere.

A properly made fruit fool is a delightful dessert. Rich and creamy, sensual and with the tang of freshness. An amazing combination of flavour and texture. I know that we are all told to cut down on fats, to beware of cholesterol and to eat fewer calories. Yes, I too feel guilty just looking at a bowl of home-made fool, but gradually I am learning an important lesson – how to give in gracefully. I reason that as I don't live solely on fool, the concepts of 'balance' and 'a sense of proportion' may be liberally applied, and fortified with this excuse I give in. Then the agonising merely shifts to a new dilemma – wondering whether or not I should allow myself a second helping!

So it's little wonder that even when you do stumble across an obscure fool recipe, it's almost always apologetic in tone. In it someone will try to convince you that you can make fool from a combination of fruit purée and thin cream. I hasten to point out that in my opinion such a fool would be hard pushed to make the grade as a pudding even at the most Dickensian of boarding schools. Fool needs to be made from three elements, each in equal proportion: fresh fruit purée, the thickest cream you can find, and a rich custard.

Thereafter it is a simple matter of adjusting the texture and taste. The texture copes well with the whizzings of a food processor, and the taste can be fine-tuned by subtle adjustment with sugar and lemon juice to perfect the sweetness/freshness balance. Then you merely have to chill the fool carefully, and work on a suitably enigmatic and unrevealing smile with which to fend off gushing compliments.

INTRODUCTION

You can make fruit fool out of anything, providing it is fruit. My personal favourites are rhubarb, gooseberry, raspberry and pear. I have set out the recipe in modular fashion because, as with many simple things, fool becomes more complicated if you turn your back on it for a second.

It is possible to make good fool without a food processor, but you have to have strong wrists and a masochistic liking for interminably pushing things through hair sieves, or winding them through a Mouli-légumes. I like my food processor and the method I have set out uses it to take the grind out of the procedure.

As mentioned earlier you need three elements. Getting the fruit purée right varies from fruit to fruit and also depends on how ripe that fruit is, so I offer some options in the method. Custard you can arrive at two ways, so I've set them both out. Finally, visit a farm and get some un-tampered-with, thick and luxurious cream.

INGREDIENTS *– for eight people*

600 ml (1 pt) fruit purée
600 ml (1 pt) custard
600 ml (1 pt) double cream

METHOD FOR THE FRUIT PURÉE

To end up with a pint of purée you will require different weights of fruit, quantities of water, and amounts of added sugar depending on which fruit you choose and the degree of ripeness of the particular crop you're using.

GUIDELINES

For a concentrated flavour use as little water as you can get away with.

Do not be nervous of ending with a thick purée.

Taste it and follow your judgement, adjust the amount of sugar until you achieve a fruity but not over-sweet taste.

Rhubarb – Pick nice pink rhubarb; it is very acidic so allow 225 g (8 oz) of granulated sugar to 1 kg (2 lb 4 oz) of rhubarb, and 100 ml (3½ fl oz) of water. Cook gently until it just breaks up.

Gooseberry – Green cooking gooseberries are best; allow 175 g (6 oz) of granulated sugar to 1 kg (2 lb 4 oz) of gooseberries, and 100 ml (3½ fl oz) of water. Top and tail the gooseberries first and then cook gently until they're well broken up.

Raspberry – Ripe but not rotten! Allow 100 g (3½ oz) of granulated sugar to 750 g (1 lb 10 oz) of raspberries. Do not cook them. Either mash them gently with a fork or use a food processor very gently!

Pears – Using dessert pears, allow 75 g (2½ oz) of granulated sugar to 1 kilo (2 lb 4 oz) of pears; if you can get cooking pears, increase the amount of sugar to 100 g (3½ oz). Use 300 ml (½ pt) of water. Peel and core the fruit, and cook gently until mushy. There's never any need to boil anything furiously – you are not making jam! Cool the purée to lukewarm before assembling the fool.

CUSTARD 1

When making fool you could get away with the cheat's custard which I've called 'Custard 2', but this recipe is for the proper stuff. The ingredients are 425 ml (15 fl oz) of whole milk, 50 g (1½ oz) of caster sugar and 4 fresh egg yolks. Heat the milk in a pan while you beat the egg yolks and sugar together until fluffy, then pour some of the nearly boiling milk on to the egg yolk mixture while you continue beating with a balloon whisk. Then pour that mixture back into the pan and continue mixing it with the rest of the hot milk. Heat very gently and soon you'll find the custard thickening to a velvet sauce. When your custard is ready, take it off and cool it. Before attempting this recipe take the time to re-read the method section of Recipe 11 – honey and ginger ice cream – where I set out the methodology of custard-making in rather more detail.

CUSTARD 2

Buy one of those jolly red, blue and yellow tins of custard powder and follow their instructions using half as much sugar as they recommend, and full-cream milk.

ASSEMBLING YOUR FOOL

When it comes to fools there are swirlers and mixers. Some folk mix the cream and custard and swirl it into the glass or bowl with swirls of fruit purée offering a contrasting colour. I like fool to be uniform in colour, taste and smoothness so I favour the 'mixer' approach.

First push your fruit purée through a sieve to remove the seeds and make it smooth. You can either mix by hand or with a blender or processor – in which case you must beware of overdoing it. The order of play is purée, then custard, then cream. When everything is uniform, adjust the taste with sugar and lemon juice until it is exactly as you want it, and then chill before serving. Whether you elect for individual glasses, or one big serving bowl, one thing is certain – this fool will be so lovely that you'll never be tempted by 'Old Mother Hubbard's Range of Genuine Country Fool-Type Desserts' again.

Number Sixteen – Once-a-Year Pudding

In which we consider King George and his
dinner on 25 December 1714

The only thing better than rummaging through second-hand books for long forgotten and gloriously impractical recipes, is what you can glean from the yellowing newspaper cuttings that sometimes fall out of them when you turn the pages. To the inquisitive, these are nearly as riveting as the old pieces of newspaper you find when you take up a carpet or reline drawers in an antique chest. Old bits of newspaper are always compulsive reading, as was the fragment I found detailing the climax of King George's Christmas dinner.

It claimed (I cannot say with what degree of accuracy) that 'King George I, who was later known as the "Pudding King", at six o'clock on Christmas Day 1714, greatly enjoyed a large Christmas pudding'.

The unknown newspaperman then went on to give the recipe, 'To make about ten pounds of pudding, take 1½ lb suet; 1 lb of eggs, weighed in their shells; 1 lb of dried plums; 1 lb of mixed peel cut into strips; 1 lb of small raisins; 1 lb of sultanas; 1 lb of currants; 1 lb of sifted flour; 1 lb of sugar; 1 lb of brown crumbs; 1 heaped teaspoonful mixed spice; ½ nutmeg grated; 2 teaspoonfuls salt; ½ pint new milk; juice of a lemon; a very large wineglassful brandy. Mix everything, stand for twelve hours, turn into buttered moulds about 3 lb to each, boil for 8 hours at first and then for two hours before serving.' Two things about this recipe are most intriguing. First, it uses about 4 eggs per pudding which is more than most modern recipes, and secondly, the ratio between the more expensive fruit and the other dry ingredients is about 6:4, which is surprisingly high considering how many bygone cooks prided themselves on being 'careful'. Perhaps the 'Pudding King' inspired an unknown chef to extravagance.

Hidden in this odd old tale is an important clue to the development of my Christmas pudding recipe. Quality tells, and that is what makes really good Christmas puddings so awesomely pricey.

If you set out with the objective of making your pudding to meet a particular quality standard – rather than adopting a less extravagant approach – it can be a chastening experience. You want to use the best ingredients – candied peel from whole fruits, fine spirits, old ales, Lexia raisins, dried apricots – but inevitably the cost of making your pud will make you blanch. That's why decent shop-bought Christmas puds end up with such monster price tags – to arrive at their selling price retailers routinely double what they pay for something. Good puddings, made from good ingredients, are not cheap even before their price has been raised by a hundred per cent. So you should never buy a Christmas pudding, but always make your own. If you make your masterpiece in September, you may even have forgotten how indulgently expensive your pudding was by the time you come to eat it at Yuletide.

After all, you only sit down to Christmas pudding once a year so you might as well make the most of it. Shut your eyes, ignore the mounting expense, and give it your best shot. You won't regret it.

INTRODUCTION

'When the going gets tough, the tough get shopping.' Making this Christmas pudding calls for some pretty tough shopping. Not everything is straightforward, and a certain amount of hunting around health food stores, delicatessens and specialist shops will repay dividends. This recipe makes enough pudding for a three-pint pudding bowl. If you fail in your mission and come up short of any of the more exotic ingredients listed here, then use your common sense and substitute something good that is easier to obtain. Your pudding will bear testimony to the effort you put into it.

INGREDIENTS

175 g (6 oz) beef suet

100 g (3½ oz) white self-raising flour

100 g (3½ oz) white breadcrumbs (fine)

225 g (8 oz) muscovado sugar

100 g (3½ oz) grated carrot

175 g (6 oz) currants

175 g (6 oz) Lexia raisins

175 g (6 oz) large sultanas

175 g (6 oz) dried apricots

50 g (1½ oz) candied lemon peel

50 g (1½ oz) candied orange peel

50 g (1½ oz) glacé ginger

50 g (1½ oz) candied angelica

100 g (3½ oz) chopped pecan nuts

100 ml (3½ fl oz) best brandy

300 ml (10 fl oz) dark, strong ale

3 large fresh eggs

The juice of half a lemon

Half of a nutmeg, grated

1 tsp ground cinnamon

½ tsp salt

SHOPPING TACTICS

Suet – Ask your butcher for a nice piece of suet from around the kidney, take it home and grate it using the finest mesh of your grater. Then dust it with a tiny bit of flour to stop it lumping together and it's ready for action.

White breadcrumbs – Hoorah for food processors! Stale white bread should be whizzed until quite fine.

Muscovado sugar – This is a different thing from demerara, it's darker and wetter.

Currants, raisins and sultanas – The overall quality of standard dried fruit has improved immeasurably over recent years. Nevertheless, try for plump currants, those large Lexia raisins, and big succulent sultanas.

Dried apricots – Get those excellent 'ready-to-eat-no-need-to-soak' ones.

Orange and lemon peel, glacé ginger, angelica – Search out an old-fashioned shop where you can still buy the whole skins of oranges and lemons or even citrons that have been candied, then slice them into fine strips, not the miserable little chunks you get in cheap packets of mixed fruit. Apply the same principles to your search for ginger and angelica.

Pecan nuts – There's nothing quite like them. Buy them halved and then chop them roughly before using them.

Best brandy – I'm afraid this means just what it says.

Ale – Before the war, every brewery in the land would make its own 'winter warmer'. High in alcohol and dark in colour, it was usually a heavy beer with good keeping potential sometimes called 'old ale'. Seek out your local brewery's most revered 'old ale' or possibly dark barley wine and use some of that. I can vouch for 'Crabber's Nip' and 'Old Peculier'. Failing that turn to stout or porter.

Nutmegs – Do invest in a nutmeg grater and use freshly grated nutmeg.

METHOD

I think that Christmas puddings are best made in September and October of the year in which they are to be eaten, because they do improve with a couple of months' keeping. In the past I have enjoyed one left over from the previous year's batch, but I could not swear to it being any great improvement on a current pudding!

So let me presume that these events take place on a pleasant autumn day. At breakfast time take the currants, raisins, sultanas and the dried apricots cut into slivers and put them to soak in the brandy for eight hours or so.

In the late afternoon peel and grate the carrots finely; prepare the breadcrumbs; shred the orange and lemon peel into long slivers the size of half a matchstick; chop the halved pecans roughly; and chop the glacé ginger and the candied angelica finely.

Beat the eggs in a jug, add the old ale and beat some more. Take all the dry ingredients, put them in your largest mixing bowl and mix thoroughly – your hands are probably the best tools for this job.

Then add the dried fruit that has been soaking in the brandy, and finally pour in the eggs and ale mixture, continuing to mix away. This is the time for all the family to gather round and wish if you are of a Dickensian persuasion.

When all is well mixed, cover the bowl with clingfilm and leave it in a cool place overnight.

The following day you will be ready for the first cooking. Pack the mixture into a well-buttered pudding bowl of about 1.8 litres (3 pints) capacity. The mixture should come no higher than within 2.5 cm (1 in) of the rim of the bowl to allow for swelling during cooking. Cover the bowl with two layers of non-stick silicone baking parchment and then a top sheet of foil and tie down securely. If you are feeling rustic then a muslin cover knotted to provide a handle for lifting the pudding is essential, otherwise attach a string harness for the purpose. Your pudding is now ready for its first boiling; it needs to be steamed for 8 hours. You can either sit it on a trivet in a large pan, or in one of those purpose-built steamers. The key principles are that the pudding basin should be surrounded by boiling water or steam for the duration, and that water shouldn't get into your pudding (i.e. don't let the water get higher than two thirds of the way up the basin). Tend it carefully, replenishing the water as necessary, because should the arrangement ever boil completely dry, the burnt pan and house full of greasy smoke that result are even more unpleasant than your wildest imaginings.

After your pudding has survived its first cooking, take it out, cool it and store it for the big day. Some cookery pundits recommend replacing the cover with a fresh one but as I don't habitually keep Christmas puddings year after year I never bother.

When your pudding's big day dawns it will need its second cooking. This takes the form of steaming as before, but this time for two and a half hours. To serve, simply turn the pudding out on to a suitable warmed plate (this is where we find out exactly how well you buttered the pudding basin in the beginning). If you'd like to march your pudding into a darkened room illuminated by its own flaring brandy you'll require an accomplice and a ladle. Get someone to walk with you with a ladle of warmed brandy, light the brandy whilst it is still in the ladle and then pour the liquid fire over the pudding at the very last minute. This will save you from having to scrabble round the pudding with a Zippo.

When you have eaten your own pudding, raise a glass to King George, think about the rigours of eighteenth-century courtly life, and as you settle back in the comfort of your central heating, relish your own extravagance.

Number Seventeen – Halibut on a Mushroom Sauce

In which we touch on the good taste of the ancient Sumerians

One of the nicest things about hosting the meetings of the Buxton Gastronomes was the range of charming and interesting speakers we got to meet. One such speaker was the beer hunter. As he introduced himself to our group, he is the Michael Jackson who neither sings nor dances. He came to Buxton to talk to us on the subject of wineglass beers, and I would have to say, at the risk of offending our other erudite and eminent speakers, that it was almost certainly the liveliest event the gastronomes ever held. The evening revolved around six different, and severely alcoholic, rare beers, and that is what surprised so many of our guests – whilst it is easy to sample six different wines and retain some sense, drinking a glass of each of six different rare, strong beers is much more debilitating. It is untrue to say that the pensioners in the party were dancing on the tables, but that is only because they no longer trusted themselves to climb up there.

As a speaker Michael Jackson did us proud. He had an awesome depth of knowledge on the subject of beer and ale, a light touch and the ability to command his audience. He opened his remarks by noting that one of the earliest civilisations – the Sumerians – had developed a hieroglyphic that stood for beer, some centuries before the earliest mention of wine. From then on, for the rest of the evening we devoted ourselves to beer and ale rather than that new young upstart wine, and a very lively evening it proved to be.

I faced the challenge of devising a menu that complemented each of these various beers and ales, and after much consultation with Michael, this was the menu we arrived at.

Menu for the October meeting of the Buxton Gastronomes

WINEGLASS BEERS

Speaker – Michael Jackson

As an Aperitif – **Lindeman's Cherry Kriek**

Scallops on the Shell
Pitfield's London Porter

Halibut on a Mushroom Sauce
Pilsner Urquell

Fillet of Lamb on a Bed of Flageolets, served with a Leek Tartlet
Biere du Gard 'Sans Culottes'

Traditional Northumbrian Plum Pudding
Imperial Russian Stout

Cheese Selection
Chimay Grand Reserve

The second course was to be a fish course that followed on from the *bonne bouche* of fresh scallops with the traditional English dark, burnt porter. The beer for this course was the strong clean-tasting Pilsner Urquell, whose fresh, almost bready, taste is most pronounced.

We needed a dish that was strongly flavoured but distinctive. It couldn't be too nutty, or oniony, and it had to be a fairly substantial to prevent this unaccustomed deluge of beer taking too much toll on empty stomachs. The halibut on a mushroom sauce attracted many compliments, and I don't think that this was solely due to the quantities of beer consumed.

INTRODUCTION

Halibut can usually be purchased in two different guises. Either as small whole fillets of white fish weighing about 200 grams (7 oz) each, or as steaks cut across the grain of a much larger fish which would have weighed upwards of one hundred kilogrammes (220 lb) to start with. The little fillets which are generally known as 'Greenland halibut' are what I used for the dinner – they are cheaper than steaks and permit easier portion control. Such is the over-fishing of these delicious fish that the huge grandmother halibut are soon likely to become a thing of the past. Like the other EC fishing fleets, we are catching the majority of halibut whilst they are still 'Greenland' sized, and very few are getting the twenty years of growth they need to turn into majestic fully grown fish. This dish will be equally successful with steaks or fillets.

Do not balk at the amount of mushrooms you need for this dish; when you buy mushrooms you are spending most of your money on water, and they will reduce down to almost nothing. Don't skimp. You are looking for a concentration of flavour. Don't go out of your way looking for perfect mushrooms either. Large, flat, open field mushrooms are fine and you'll get a nice dark sauce against which the clean white of the fish will look very good.

INGREDIENTS (sauce quantities for four)
   Allow 2 nice fillets of halibut, or one larger steak, per person
   100 g (3 ½ oz) best unsalted butter
   100 g (3½ oz) very finely chopped onion
   500 g (1 lb 2 oz) flat mushrooms
   284 ml carton of double cream
   Ground black pepper and salt

METHOD
First make your sauce, which is a fairly lengthy procedure. Chop the mushrooms up fairly finely – stalks, caps, peel and all. Take a large pan – a wok is ideal for this if you have one – and melt the butter in it. Add the onions and the mushrooms and cook very slowly. After fifteen minutes or

so, the water will start to leach out of the mushrooms. Keep on, merely giving an occasional stir to stop everything sticking. Then gradually increase the heat until you have driven off all the water and you are left with a much smaller amount of concentrated mushroom and onion sludge. Transfer this sludge to your trusty food processor and whizz it. When the mushrooms and onion have been liquidised, add the cream and turn it off (you must be careful not to beat the cream into butter). Transfer it all to a clean saucepan and cook your fish.

To cook the halibut place each fillet on a sheet of buttered foil and wrap it up tightly. Steam the parcels until the fish is cooked – i.e. firm to the touch when you press it with your finger.

Warm the sauce (which will look more like a smooth purée) through and add salt and pepper; it will probably need quite a lot of salt. Do not let the sauce boil. Then pour a lavish pool of sauce on to each plate, and unwrap the fish and sit each piece or pair of fillets on top of the sauce. For the sake of adventure accompany it with a glass of the original Pilsner Urquell – an elegant combination of flavours.

Number Eighteen – Chinese Caramel Ice Cream

In which Switzerland joins forces with
Kwangtung Province

For a few weeks of the year Buxton goes potty. At some point, veiled in the mists of time, Buxton decided that it would hold a yearly opera festival and so show off its magnificent Opera House. One thing led to another and the festival grew into a celebration of rarer operas. This was a stroke of marketing genius because it meant that each year one item on the programme would either be very rare or even unperformed. So for real opera buffs the Buxton Festival became a unique opportunity to see operas that would otherwise be languishing in dusty archives somewhere, and that opportunity guaranteed ticket sales. On the other hand, the reason why these operas had either been infrequently, or never, performed before tended to be because the operas were no good. So in a nutshell Buxton made sure of its audience, but it was an audience comprised of people going out of their way to see pretty suspect operas, and some of them were very odd people indeed.

No wonder Buxton hoteliers viewed the festival with only qualified enthusiasm. The town was certainly busy; hotels were certainly full; it is just that the visitors weren't like normal visitors. Suddenly cravats and bow ties blossomed everywhere, tweeds and goatee beards, irritable elderly ladies with irritable elderly dogs. Rare opera meant filling the town with rare people.

At our place we used quite to enjoy the festival. We offered our customers 'split-dinners'. I always maintain that eating dinner before the theatre at six o'clock leads inevitably to slumber in the second act, whilst waiting until half-past ten and the final curtain before starting dinner means a night made sleepless by persistent indigestion. So the plan was this: guests would arrive at six o'clock, park their cars and enjoy a bottle of wine and the first course of their dinner, then they'd order their main course and a coach would whisk them down to the opera. At the close of the piece the coach would bring them back up the hill to the hotel where their pre-ordered main course would be ready for them.

This all went swimmingly until the night of the extra encores.

Thirty-five covers all exactly thirty minutes late; a bit of excitement front of house; a waitress in tears; a couple of people who disputed what they had ordered. In short – chaos. We had a nice couple staying who were the kind of enthusiastic diners that gladden a chef's heart, but they ended up bearing the brunt of our troubles. The only way to make amends was by giving the gentleman three portions of this caramel ice cream. In fact it proved to have such a calming influence, that a month or so later, his wife rang up for the recipe.

This recipe is one of those curious phenomena that combines simple ingredients, patience and guile to produce a texture and taste that is outrageously delicious. There's nothing very subtle about the ingredients: sugar, eggs, cream, milk and vanilla pods. If you have an ice cream machine it's not even very hard work. But it is excruciatingly delicious. I think the cook's task is made considerably easier by using raw Chinese sugar. So as the Chinese are reputed to have given us gunpowder it only seems fair to give them a credit for this ice cream in return!

The method used to make this ice cream does mean that the egg yolks do not get 'cooked' and so you may wish to use pasteurised egg yolks or even turn the page and make some other dish! I am careful where I get my eggs from, choosing producers whose flocks are regularly tested for salmonella. I don't keep ice cream or mayonnaise hanging around for weeks after I have made it. And I always explain the situation to anyone I invite to share such things. But I do use unpasteurised eggs. I am not a frail old-age pensioner, pregnant mother or tiny infant, and I choose to take my chances. It's a calculated risk: the taste of real ice cream versus the possibility of a dose of food poisoning.

INTRODUCTION

Generally I like to avoid dishes that hinge upon exotic ingredients, and I should make it clear that this ice cream can be made using white sugar. The objective is to melt the sugar until it becomes a delicate golden brown and will give a gentle caramely taste to the ice cream. Heat it just a tiny bit too far and your finished ice will taste bitter and burnt. Getting it just right is a very delicate manoeuvre.

The rock, or yellow lump, sugar you can buy from Chinese super-markets has more taste than white, highly refined sugar and lends itself to this caramel-making exercise. With a tricky task like this one, anything that makes the cook's life a bit easier is to be welcomed, so if you can get some I'd recommend you do so.

In addition I must confess to being completely won over by the man who writes the copy for the boxes on behalf of the 'China National Cereals, Oils and Foodstuffs Import and Export Corporation, Kwang-tung Province, People's Republic of China'. His telling prose runs as follows and this extract keeps faith with the original: 'Rock Sugar (yellow lump) is a famous product of Kwangtung province. It is purely processed from choice sugar cane after traditional method, clear and bright, pure and sweet. It is much appreciated by consumers at home and abroad.' I agree wholeheartedly; see if you can get hold of some.

INGREDIENTS

3 whole vanilla pods – only the real thing will do I'm afraid. For choice, those branded 'Bourbon' from the Île de Réunion.
225 g (8 oz) Chinese yellow rock sugar
284 ml carton fresh double cream

300 ml (10 fl oz) Jersey milk
8 fresh egg yolks

METHOD

This is difficult to get just right; it will be easier with the chunky Chinese sugar. First of all, split your vanilla pods lengthwise and scrape the seeds out into a large thick-bottomed pan. This pan has to be able to take a lot of heat. Then put the sugar in and heat gradually. It is virtually impossible to do this too slowly! If you rush, the sugar will quite suddenly go from being solid to a black burnt liquid. Patience is the key and you shouldn't worry if it takes you half an hour. Keep getting your pan, and the sugar in it, a bit hotter and then a little bit more until quite suddenly it becomes liquid. Then you should proceed even more cautiously until it is a golden brown liquid. Take the pan off the heat and add the cream. There is no way to avoid the splutters and fizzes at this point, so be careful. Put it back on a very gentle heat until the caramel has dissolved into the cream. Then take the mixture off the heat. Heat the milk to just below boiling point in a second saucepan while you lightly whisk the egg yolks to break them up. Pour the cooling milk into the egg yolks a bit at a time to make a custard, whilst beating with a balloon whisk to avoid curdling. Amalgamate this custard with the caramel cream. Whisk together thoroughly and leave to go cold. Then strain your caramel custard to remove the vanilla pods, pop it into your ice cream machine and tally-ho! This makes a pretty heavy mixture, so don't overfill your machine.

The result is a simple and luxurious ice cream best enjoyed on its own.

Number Nineteen – Chestnut Soup

In which we consider the impact
of sous vide *on fingers*

There's a striking Georgian square that overlooks the racecourse in Worcester, and in the middle of it is an elegant girls' school set amongst green velvet lawns and tennis courts. Around the boundary stands a perimeter of magnificent old trees with their branches almost roofing-in the roadway. Every October this square becomes a Mecca for small boys of all ages – not, I hasten to point out, because of the proximity of the girls' school, but due to the profusion of horse-chestnut trees and conkers. Conkers so highly prized that it's a wonder they even manage to hit the ground before being swept away to be pickled or baked and then going on to new careers as 'oners', 'twoers', and so forth. Anyhow, by way of a contrast, a few weeks later the Spanish chestnut trees ripen, and plump sweet chestnuts rain to the ground to be universally ignored. After another week or so the whole harvest has been mashed on to the roadway by passing cars and there is nothing to show for it but pinkish smears on the tarmac. Only the English could be so profoundly suspicious of free food, and only the English could remain stubbornly unaware of how tasty chestnuts can be.

My mother used to enjoy a certain notoriety for the excellence of her chestnut stuffing. It was a novelty that crowned the Christmas turkey. It also involved the family in the Christmas Eve ordeal. Whilst other more devout families were preparing themselves for midnight Mass on Christmas Eve, the Campions were usually burning their fingers trying to peel the chestnuts for this wonderful stuffing. Every cookbook has a suggestion as to how to peel chestnuts and all these tips have one thing in common – they are a lot more plausible than they are effective.

My mother's recipe for chestnut stuffing (forty chestnuts, parboiled, then peeled, then roughly chopped; 225 g [8 oz] onions, chopped, fried in butter until transparent, and cooled; 350 g [12 oz] good quality butcher's pork sausage meat [see Recipe 36, page 215, for further observations on the vexed subject of sausage meat]; about 125 g [4½ oz] fresh white breadcrumbs; a beaten egg; a large bunch of fresh parsley, chopped finely; plenty of ground black pepper; mix well with your hands until homogeneous and then stuff into the neck end of the turkey) produced a really nice stuffing with a good texture to it. But every Christmas Eve somebody had to sit and try to peel the chestnuts while they were still hot from the pan. Burnt fingers were guaranteed, as tinned chestnuts just would not do. Clement Faugier market tinned chestnuts in various guises, and whilst they are suitable for patisserie work they just don't have the taste or texture needed for savoury dishes. Enter the new technology, and a plastic tray of whole, peeled chestnuts vacuum-packed *sous vide*. A reputable brand name to look out for is Ponthier. These chestnuts taste great; the texture compares well with fresh chestnuts; and there are no burnt fingers involved. This is a wonderful product, and invigorated by the thought of avoiding the ordeal by chestnut peeling, I developed this recipe for a chestnut soup that is simple, rich, filling and very tasty.

INTRODUCTION

The quality of your finished chestnut soup will depend almost entirely on the quality of the chestnuts you start out with. Fresh is best, as always, and if you can stomach the parboiling and peeling rituals that's the way to proceed. The French chestnuts that have been peeled and vacuum-packed in plastic trays are jolly nearly as good as fresh, and do not involve you in any peeling. As a third option there are the whole unsweetened chestnuts which have been tinned in water. Chestnut paste; chestnut purée; chestnut cream; chestnuts in vanilla syrup – I am afraid none of them will do.

In the France of the eighteenth and nineteenth centuries, chestnut flour was often used by people too poor to afford wheat as the basis of bread, and this gives some indication of the starchy properties of these much maligned nuts. This starchiness means that the chestnuts make this soup a very thick and rich one. To counter any accusations of blandness I would suggest serving it with a 'garnish' of a few shreds of salty home-cured bacon that have been fried until shrapnel crisp. The smooth sweet soup contrasts perfectly with these savoury morsels.

INGREDIENTS

500 g vacuum pack of natural chestnuts

350 g (12 oz) finely chopped onions

1 litre (1¾ pints) skimmed milk

50 g (1¾ oz) unsalted butter

Salt and freshly ground black pepper

METHOD

This is almost embarrassingly easy! Sweat the onions in the butter to drive the water out of them, but do not allow them to colour. Add the chestnuts and skimmed milk, and simmer until all is very soft. Whizz in a food processor or liquidiser thoroughly until perfectly smooth. Depending on just how thick you like your soups to be you can let the chestnut mixture down with a little more milk. Adjust the seasoning with salt and pepper (bearing in mind that if you propose to add some crispy bits of salty bacon when serving, you'll need to hold back a little on the salting at this stage). Return the soup to the pan, heat, serve, and eat with gusto.

Number Twenty – Onion Sauce and Bread Sauce

*In which we discuss the delicacies known
during my childhood as 'delicious cold'*

When I was a child my father used to run a small company whose business he always described as import–export. I don't know just what it was they dealt in, but I do know that it meant my mother having to cook for a succession of foreign buyers and sellers on their visits to Britain. She had one banker, never fail, dish – roast lamb and onion sauce. And it was the onion sauce that turned the trick. Only a very few of our guests were familiar with a shoulder of lamb and the accompanying shrapnel-crisp roast potatoes; almost none of them had ever tasted onion sauce before. Her excellent bread sauce generally only made an appearance at Christmas but it was built along the same lines.

Both these sauces were known by my father as 'delicious cold', and when a succession of puzzled foreigners would ask why this was so he would simply roar with laughter and say that it was because that's just what they were.

In this respect he was absolutely right. But only when we are talking about a proper onion or bread sauce that is rich enough to slice when cold. Somewhere along the line most cooks seem to have fallen under the misapprehension that onion sauce is made by sticking an onion with a couple of cloves, bathing it in milk, fishing it out and then thickening up the perfumed milk.

If your sauce is to be called onion sauce then surely it should taste of onions? I like onions, so I don't mind if bread sauce is redolent of onions too. The nicest thing you can say about the tasteless pap that masquerades as bread sauce on tables throughout the land, is that it is so dull as to make accountancy seem exciting.

As usual Mrs Beeton had a hand in it. Her recipe for onion sauce is made by taking white sauce and adding two chopped cooked onions; she doesn't say how they've been cooked but references to the 'liquor in which the onions were cooked' leave a dark suspicion that they were boiled.

Paul Bocuse makes a better fist of it with his recipe for sauce soubise, which is a combination of bèchamel sauce and sautéed onions, but he still boiled the onions for a minute before sautéeing them.

For goodness sake, let's have sauces that taste richly of what they're supposed to taste of. And if they're rich enough to slice when cold then they can play an important role in a classic turkey sandwich – well and truly 'delicious cold'.

INTRODUCTION

I have placed these two sauces together because, to my way of thinking, they are the same sauce thickened differently. In the case of bread sauce, rather naturally the thickening agent is white bread-crumbs. Fortunately – with the advent of food processors – there is no longer any need for someone to sit at the kitchen table and rub stale white bread and the skin off their knuckles through a grater. Simply get the white middle of a three- or four-day-old loaf and whizz it in the processor. Whizz it finely, as this will have an influence on the texture of the final sauce. If you use much staler bread it will thicken too much, any fresher and it won't thicken enough. Packet breadcrumbs are a waste of both your time and your money.

For onion sauce I suggest thickening the sauce the quick way, with what is usually referred to in professional kitchens as 'fecule' – potato flour. You can use cornflour if you want, but it advertises your short cut with a metallic taste and a slippery texture. Potato flour is increasingly available from specialist food shops and shops selling Asian produce. It is pure starch, quick and easy to use, and relatively blunder-proof.

INGREDIENTS FOR ONION SAUCE

750 g (1 lb 10 oz) strong onions
110 g (4 oz) unsalted butter
500 ml (nearly 1 pt) milk

Freshly ground black pepper
Pounded mace
284 ml carton double cream
2 tbs potato flour
Salt

METHOD FOR ONION SAUCE

I don't want my sauce perfectly white. So no lemon juice, pre-boiling of the onions, or other fiddle-faddles. I like the slight creamy colour of the onions, the flecks of black pepper and the orange specks of mace.

Peel and chop the onions. Chop them so that they are in about 1 cm (½ in) dice. Melt the butter in a heavy frying pan, toss the onions in it and cook gently until they are transparent. Then add the milk. Three or four turns of freshly ground black pepper and a good pinch of mace (at this point you have to decide by trial and error how strong a presence of mace you're after. I love it. It tastes like a well-tempered nutmeg.). Then turn the flame down and let everything simmer along very slowly for half an hour, with a lid on if you have one that fits. Try and avoid curdling the milk by letting everything get too hot, but don't worry if it gets away from you, as the fecule will see you right in the end. When you start to dish up the rest of the meal, finish the sauce. Slake the potato flour in a little water and add the resulting liquid to the sauce, turning the heat up at the same time. Then cook until the starch has converted and the sauce is thick. Exactly how much fecule you use will depend on how thick you like your sauce. But remember, this sauce is delicious cold and a stiffer sauce will set better. Finally beat in the cream and add salt to taste, and warm through carefully. Do not salt the sauce at an earlier stage than this or the salty taste will 'cook-in' and get stronger than you had bargained for.

METHOD FOR BREAD SAUCE

Use the same ingredients but exclude the potato flour and make some white breadcrumbs. About as many as you'd get from attacking the crumb part of a large white loaf with a food processor.

Then follow the same plan as for onion sauce but start the whole procedure much earlier, as making bread sauce takes an hour longer than making onion sauce. Carry on until the point where you would be adding the cream and the potato flour for thickening. Transfer the sauce, without adding the cream yet, to a double saucepan and gradually stir in half the breadcrumbs. Put the lid on and let it simmer away happily, just giving it the occasional stir. Once again, judgement is called for in deciding just how thick you let it get. With breadcrumbs it is a much more gradual process than with starch so don't be impatient, add more breadcrumbs a little at a time. When you think it is about right, desist. When you're absolutely ready to serve, add salt to the sauce – it tends to need a bit more than you would put in onion sauce because of the blandness of the bread, and then beat the cream in to let it down a little. Leave it to warm through. Then enjoy it thoroughly. Turkey, chicken or sausages all make perfectly good excuses to enjoy this delight.

And you'll find that it does live up to its billing: it's delicious cold.

Number Twenty-One – Mrs Campion's Chocolate Pudding

In which we worry a good deal about the
problems of greed

The last knockings of the twentieth century were the chocolate years. Never can a food have been so perfectly in tune with the dominant refrain of British society. Not only were we encouraged to 'get rich quick', we were given the all-clear to be greedy in every way we could. 'Death by chocolate', 'chocolate truffle cake', 'Mississippi mud pie', were all marketed to diners who attacked them greedily. And these were dishes so rich that if faced with them my grandmother would have hitched up her stays and launched into a strident homily about the links between excess and boils.

At our restaurant we played our part in this celebration of chocolate: Mrs Campion's chocolate pudding took pride of place on our dessert menu. It is such an incredibly moreish chocolate dessert that elderly ladies sometimes refused their first course in order to be certain that they would have more room when pudding came around. On the menu I described it as 'very chocolate' and that terminology still holds good. The origins of this pudding lie in a series of dinner parties we held long before the hotel and restaurant were even a twinkle in our fevered imagination. My wife, endlessly patient with my usurping her kitchen for showing off at dinner parties, demanded that the pudding course be left to her. She devised this dish, a torte-cum-truffle-cum-cake that took no prisoners. All I did was mess with the presentation and fiddle with the concept.

In essence this is a layered pudding. Reading from the floor up, it goes like this: first a layer of chocolate sponge cake painted until soggy with brandy; then a layer of dark chocolate ganache; then a layer of white chocolate ganache; then a dusting of bitter cocoa powder. The whole edifice to be put together in a flan ring (either a 30 cm [12 in] one, or eight individual 8 cm [3 ½ in] rings), then chilled.

It's a shattering fact that much of the confectionery described as chocolate, and sold on the mass market in the UK, doesn't even merit the name chocolate when assessed by the standards of the purist chocoholic. Fortunately the supermarkets and specialist food shops have spotted our increasing choco-sophistication and now 70-per-cent-cocoa dark chocolate is available in a variety of guises.

Buying good white chocolate also presents a problem, although strictly speaking white chocolate is not really chocolate at all, as it never contains any cocoa, merely cocoa butter. It is, as the French rather disparagingly put it, a *produit de laboratoire*. When buying white chocolate your problem is a slightly different one. You're seeking something that won't immediately remind all your diners of the Milky

Bar Kid – and that can be more difficult than you might suppose. Brand names worth searching for are Lindt, and Green & Black; recently some of the grander supermarket chains have started to offer their own white chocolate for cooking which seems sound.

INTRODUCTION

As if searching for the right kind of chocolate is not enough, I am afraid that for complete mastery of this pudding you could really do with some simple but esoteric equipment. I call them flan rings but they are not. They come in a variety of sizes, but the principles are the same – they are plain circular collars made from stainless steel about 3 mm ($\frac{1}{16}$ in) thick. Each stands about 4.5 cm (2 in) deep, and you can either use several, each with a diameter of about 8 cm (3 in), or one with a diameter of about 30 cm (12 in). You use these rings to cut the sponge base from your sheet of sponge cake, then you pack them with the two ganache layers, then you chill everything. When you come to serve dessert, you wrestle the finished pudding from the ring, sprinkle the top with cocoa and then pop it on to a virgin plate. It is also important to make sure that you obtain white and dark chocolate, and indeed cocoa powder, of the highest possible quality. Nowhere have I mentioned drinking chocolate, and that's because it simply won't do!

INGREDIENTS

Please take this section as giving you accurate proportions for the ingredients concerned. Obviously quantities will need to be adjusted to suit the precise size of ring (or rings) you are working with. These quantities are sufficient to make eight individual portions in small rings.

FOR THE CHOCOLATE SPONGE:

75 g (2½ oz) white self-raising flour

75 g (2½ oz) unsalted butter

75 g (2½ oz) caster sugar

2 large fresh eggs

1 heaped tbs cocoa powder

1 tsp baking powder

1 small glass brandy

FOR THE GANACHE:

1 litre (1¾ pints) whipping cream

250 g (9 oz) high-quality bitter chocolate

325 g (11½ oz) high-quality white chocolate

25 g (1 oz) high-quality cocoa powder

METHOD FOR THE CHOCOLATE SPONGE BASE

Take your trusty food processor, pop in the butter, sugar and eggs, then whizz them until they're a fluffy sludge. Add the flour and cocoa and finally the baking powder. Whizz some more until well mixed, then add some warm water a little bit at a time, until the mixture is the consistency of thick Yorkshire pudding batter. Then put a piece of non-stick silicone baking parchment on to a baking sheet and pour out your mixture so that it makes a puddle about 5 mm thick. Bake it in a pre-heated oven – gas mark 3 / 325°F / 160°C for about fifteen minutes. Because of the role it is to play in the rest of this recipe it doesn't matter if this is not a sponge so light and fluffy that it would win cups at village shows. Equally if you have no food processor do not despair, simply look at the method I have given here and do your best to replicate it with a bowl and beater of some kind.

When the sponge is cooked, put it – still on its paper – on to a rack and let it cool.

When cool, turn it over so that the shiny side is down and peel off the paper. Then, using the rings as cutters, punch out circles of sponge and leave them lodged in the rings. Take a pastry brush and paint the sponge base in each ring with the brandy until pleasantly soggy. Keep every-thing cool.

METHOD FOR THE GANACHE

Take your time over this, chocolate hates being rushed. You need to set up a bain-marie for melting your chocolate: simply wedge a bowl in the steam over a saucepan of boiling water, and pop the dark chocolate in to melt slowly. Meanwhile beat the cream until it is half whipped – that is to say thickening up. Take half the cream and fold it into the dark chocolate away from the heat, mix until all is homogeneous and the colour is uniform. Then half fill each ring with the dark ganache, smooth down with the back of a spoon and pop in the fridge. About half an hour later, repeat the procedure with the remaining half of the cream and the white chocolate, this time filling the rings to the top and levelling them off with the back of a knife. Put them into the fridge to chill for several hours.

PRESENTATION

Before serving, take the puddings out of the fridge and whilst they are still in the rings use a tea strainer to sprinkle a dusting of cocoa powder on to their white top layers. Then push them up from the bottom of the rings, to get them out in one piece. You should end up with eight perfect little Mrs Campion's chocolate puddings. If you have made one large one, getting the pudding out of the ring can prove rather more exciting than one would wish! Warming the ring with a hot cloth can help, but individual ones are easier. Take heart though, with Mrs Campion's chocolate puddings, even your most tragic-looking mistakes will still taste absolutely delicious!

Number Twenty-Two – Taglierini with Wild Mushrooms

In which even the mushrooms
are driven to drink

It was a challenge to gastronauts everywhere. When we had the hotel we felt obliged to put steak on the menu as a banker choice for anyone feeling too unadventurous to stray into the heady reaches of cassoulet and grilled red snapper. And why not? On a recent trip to France I found myself enjoying steak and chips in a Parisian eating house; as I did so, I stopped to wonder at the motivation for travelling all that way to have something plain – especially when surrounded by other tempting, more ambitious delicacies. But then I looked down at the plate: lean red meat, grilled crisp outside, still very rare inside and frites that were thin, and so crisp that they whispered as you spooned them out. Enough philosophy, I thought, what about dinner!

If I may quote from our old menu on the subject of steak: 'Usually rump, but sometimes sirloin or porterhouse if they offer better quality at the butcher's on the day. A ten-ounce steak cooked as you wish, and served plain grilled or with a shallot sauce. (If you would prefer a larger steak, please come out to the kitchen and we will cut you one and price it on the spot.)'

The point being that you can never have anything better than exactly what you want. One of our regular customers was an eminent medical man of the larger sort, and he displayed an ability as trencherman that would gladden the heart of even the most misanthropic of chefs. He quite often succumbed to the challenge and asked for a 'decent-sized steak', and I used to respond by sending him out an exquisite lump of top-quality meat, but one that would need to be measured in pounds rather than ounces. I confess that I never succeeded in over-facing him, although I once came close by dint of cheating.

My finest hour, and the closest I got to seeing anything come back on Tim's dinner plate, was the occasion on which he had the taglierini with wild mushrooms as a starter. This is a delicious and deceptively filling dish, and in order to aid and abet my chances in the great steak challenge I sent him out a fairly stern issue of pasta and wild mushrooms by way of a first course, knowing full well that he would be unable to just pick at it, and would thus handicap himself considerably.

Fortunately his appetite was more than a match for our cuisine despite this subterfuge, but this superb and simple dish is the only one that ever got me close to success in our gastronomic duels. When it comes to mushrooms the Italians think we're barking mad. The country-side of England is littered with delicious wild mushrooms. Mushrooms which we all avoid because we have been taught as children that toadstools are poisonous. Walk in the New Forest in the autumn and mingle with the furtive Italian restaurateurs who are gazumping the English mushroom crop. They take the spoils home and dry them. You see, they all know that dried mushrooms are particularly tasty – the process of drying them out and then re-hydrating them breaks down the cell walls and allows the flavours to develop to their full potential in a most impressive way. Fortunately you can get dried mushrooms in various supermarkets and delicatessens. Look out for *mélange forestière*, which will probably be a random mixture of *ceps, girolles, trompettes de la mort* and *mousserons*, any and all of which are delicious.

Dehydrated mushrooms tend to weigh five times their weight when successfully revived so you'll only need a couple of ounces of dried. If you can lay your hand on something with which to blackmail an Italian mushroom hunter out of his spoils better still. The other key to making this dish so delicious is to rehydrate your dried mushrooms carefully in a mixture of equal parts of water and sweet sherry. This gives an added dimension to the flavour.

INTRODUCTION

On your shopping list you have two major elements: the mushrooms and the pasta. I have already touched on the mushrooms. As to the pasta, if you make your own and you are both proud of it and confident, then use it. It needs to take the form of ribbons about 4 mm wide. If you are buying pasta, choose pasta that looks like it is the right size. Don't rely on the name taglierini, or taglioni, or taglieretta as they vary from brand to brand; keep looking out for plain egg pasta that conforms to the size and shape you have in mind. Bear in mind that the Italians always rate top-quality dried pasta ahead of so-so freshly made. Frankly, I do not choose to spend a great deal of time striving with pasta only to arrive at a home-made end product that is no nicer than the shop-bought stuff.

INGREDIENTS

50 g (½ oz) mixed dried wild mushrooms

150 ml (5 fl oz) sweet sherry

175 g (6 oz) very finely chopped onions

50 ml (2 fl oz) good olive oil

50 g (1½ oz) unsalted butter

500 g pasta – fine ribbons

Salt and freshly ground black pepper

METHOD

About an hour before you want to eat, wash the dried mushrooms carefully to get rid of grit and stones, then put them in a pudding basin with the sherry and four fluid ounces of warm water. Ten minutes before the off, chop the onions finely and cook them very, very slowly in a frying pan with the oil and the butter. Five minutes before meal time add the contents of the pudding basin – by now the mushrooms will have soaked up nearly all the liquid – to the pan and fry quickly to drive off any remaining water. Season, being particularly enthusiastic with the salt to balance the sweetness of the sherry. Put the pasta into a large quantity of boiling salted water and cook as per the maker's instructions – or five minutes or so. Then strain your pasta and add the mushroom gunge; mix thoroughly and serve quickly.

After the pasta, see if you fancy a large steak!

Number Twenty-Three – Spiced-Olive-Oil Cake

*In which we get the measure of
polyunsaturated*

When it comes to nit-picking, the lawyer-like people who check out the suitability of television commercial scripts could give the masterclass. Television commercials are supposed to start by being legal, honest, decent and truthful, and then go on to comply with a whole host of other complicated rules. In a past incarnation as an advertising copy-writer, I once had a catfood script turned down, for using the line 'Cats know what's good for them' – the lady with the all-important rubber stamp justified this decision by pointing out that you could poison a cat, and therefore they didn't always know what was good for them. She then went on to suggest that they would be happy for us to say, 'Cats know it's [and in context this rather perplexingly meant our product] good for them.' And those were the words that finally graced the nation's television screens.

A particularly knotty forest of television pedantry grew up around the term polyunsaturates. For a while polyunsaturates were seen by the consumer as having magical powers; nobody understood exactly what they did, but everybody wanted them to do it. Something this wonderful just had to be protected, and in the end it was decreed that you were not allowed to say 'high in polyunsaturates' unless you were also able to say 'low in saturates': you couldn't have one without the other.

Anyhow, one of the key 'good guys' was olive oil, and the stage was set for the gradual and health-promoting change away from hard fats to polyunsaturates. On the supermarket shelves we now see margarines, and spreads, and half-butters, and 'pro-biotic' spreads that do you good, and solid oils for frying in – the chemist's lab has altered our perspective on what you need for a particular job. But of all these variants olive oil is still the one that tastes best. So why not use olive oil to replace the fat element in cake making?

This spiced-olive-oil cake was a response to that query, and it works! The end product is a rich-tasting cake that leans towards the solid rather than the airy-fairy end of the lightness spectrum, and is none the worse for that. My children love it, and whilst it is probably not as good for them as insisting that they make do with yet another piece of fruit, it is probably better for them than a more conventional cake.

INTRODUCTION
It has to be admitted that I am besotted with the flavour of good olive oil, so may I suggest this strategy – if you agree, then use a luxurious,

deep green, extra virgin oil; and if you're not so keen, use a more innocuous 'ordinary' olive oil. Do get yourself a nutmeg grater and fresh nutmegs, as the taste will be a revelation. And do look out for nice plump Australian sultanas, they make a real difference. This recipe also calls for a modicum of forethought to get the pre-soaking under way in time; it is no disaster if you don't manage it, but it does help.

INGREDIENTS

160 ml (6 fl oz) good olive oil
1 tsp freshly grated nutmeg
1 tsp ground cinnamon
125 ml (4 fl oz) tea without milk
275 g (9½ oz) Australian sultanas
350 g (12 oz) self-raising flour
275 g (9½ oz) demerara sugar
2 large fresh eggs
1 heaped tsp baking powder

METHOD

About twelve hours or so before you are to start baking, start soaking! Put the olive oil in a jug and stir into it the cinnamon and the freshly grated nutmeg. Put a bit of clingfilm over the top and set it to one side. Then take the black tea and soak the sultanas in it.

At baking time, take your trusty food processor and start by whizzing the flour and sugar together. Then add the spiced oil and the eggs – which you have previously whipped together in a mug. Then add the baking powder and finally the sultanas. Whizz slowly, and very briefly – long enough to distribute the sultanas evenly, but not so long that you chop them up.

Pour the mixture into a cake tin that you have already lined with a disc of silicone baking parchment for the base and a strip running around the sides. I recommend a round tin with a removable base (21 cm or 8 in diameter and 8 cm or 3 in deep). The silicone paper should stand proud of the top of the cake tin by about 7 cm (2½ in) to help avoid burning the top of the cake. Set the oven at gas mark 3 / 325°F / 160°C. The cake should take between an hour and three quarters and two hours, so check it after an hour and a half. When it is done take the cake from the tin and let it cool, still wrapped in its baking parchment, on a rack.

Number Twenty-Four – Sweetbreads in Parsley and Onion Sauce

In which we touch on the unpredictability of the restaurant trade

It's always the same when diners first spot sweetbreads on the menu. However knowledgeable and sophisticated they may be, there's an intake of breath and occasionally a little light giggling. Thereafter they diverge into two groups, those who love offal and those who loathe it.

I count myself lucky that during my childhood we were given all manner of offal to eat in the day-to-day course of events. Sweetbreads were elevated to the status of 'a treat', as they were a particular favourite of my father. I have a clear recollection of a dish of *Rís de Veau Forestière* which I enjoyed at Chez Solange during an outing to London when I was about twelve. Sadly Chez Solange is now long gone but that memory is the template against which I judge all sweetbread dishes. I am delighted to say that this recipe for sweetbreads in a parsley and onion sauce passes with flying colours.

When you ask for sweetbreads in the butcher's shop – given that the rest of the queue don't snigger ignorantly (and that the butcher has any to sell) – ask him just what is it that you are buying? It is time to put our cards on the table. Sweetbreads are glands – they can be pancreas, thyroid or testicle; the majority tend to come from sheep or calves; and they can also be called fry, or heartbreads.

Generally the *ris de veau* you come across on menus is the pancreas of a calf, whilst lamb's fry is likely to be lamb's testicles. Once during a rather wild Cretan holiday, our party – which consisted of a group of hardened bachelors from the rugby club – saw a menu board bearing the legend *Pigs Ball*. Aha, we thought, perhaps this will turn out to be a meatball made of pork? Still uncertain, we read the title of the same dish in its Greco-Spanish translation – *Testículos dos Porcos*. This left little room for confusion. Ever audacious, we volunteered one of our number to try it.

Fortunately, in addition to being an excellent cook, Don is a gastronomic adventurer, and to give him credit, he not only tried this delicacy but he also inspected it raw – so as to know more clearly what he was getting himself into. Uncooked it looked rather like a cricket ball that quivered; cooked it was tough, and when I tried a morsel, I found it a bit too piggy for my taste. All in all, not the kind of delicacy that demands repeating, unlike sweetbreads in a parsley and onion sauce, which is such a splendid dish that I even put it on our restaurant menu.

Selling sweetbreads to the Derbyshire dining public was an ambitious and unpredictable enterprise. I recall that throughout the first week, no one ordered the dish. Midway through the second week we had one of those dead nights, and faced with the prospect of throwing away yet another batch of splendid sweetbreads I sat the staff down and we ate the lot. (The pot washer put on a particularly fine three-helping display of freestyle eating, after overcoming his initial prejudices and actually tasting his first sweetbread.) In the following three days, four lots of diners asked for sweetbreads, only to be told that 'unfortunately we have just run out'.

INTRODUCTION

To cook sweetbreads you must first buy some, and this is not a corner-shop or cheap supermarket mission. You will probably need to enlist the support of your butcher, and that butcher will probably need to be one of the more old-fashioned upmarket variety. Demanding fresh sweetbreads at the meat section of a modern supermarket, or even in those butcher's shops that are merely links in a national chain, is almost certain to be doomed to failure or those giggles and grimaces the word sweetbread tend to inspire. Try butchers you know, try specialists, and, I'm afraid to say, try those butchers with a reputation for being expensive. What you want is fresh calf's pancreas, but the dish will work with any of the other bits and pieces that are known by the description of sweetbreads. The other vital ingredient is fresh parsley . . . dark green, curly, English parsley.

INGREDIENTS

500 g (1 lb 2 oz) fresh sweetbreads

225 g (8 oz) chopped onions

25 g (1 oz) finely chopped parsley

50 g (1½ oz) unsalted butter

600 ml (1 pint) whole milk

142 ml carton double cream

2 tbs potato flour – or cornflour as second best

Salt and freshly ground black pepper

Ground mace

METHOD

Having got your sweetbreads, pop them into a large bowl of clean cold water and leave them to soak for half an hour. Drain and repeat the operation three times. Then prepare a large saucepan full of boiling water with a splash of vinegar in it, rather as if you were about to poach eggs. Put the sweetbreads in for one minute and then lift them out into a large bowl of cold clean water as before. This blanching will allow you to give them a thorough going over. You should strip off the tougher outer membranes, also any odd-looking gobs of fat, pipes or tubes that are attached. It's hard to be precise, as just what you should remove varies from sweetbread to sweetbread, but as a general guide when you've finished, the bits you have left should be in largish pieces and everything should be edible. You'll know when you have succeeded because all your diners will have spotlessly clean plates.

Put the sweetbreads to one side and put the butter and onions into a heavy frying pan over a low heat; you need to sweat them until they are soft without any browning. Then add a good pinch of mace and the finely chopped parsley and then the milk. Do not salt anything yet. Transfer the sweetbreads and the sauce to a medium-sized casserole (about 2 litres in capacity). Place it in an oven set at gas mark 4 / 350°F / 180°C – for an hour. Then take the pot out of the oven and very carefully strain all the liquid off into a saucepan, putting the casserole of sweetbreads back in the oven to keep warm. First use the potato flour to thicken the sauce to your liking, then use the cream to smooth it, and finally add salt and black pepper to season it. Then put the sauce and the sweetbreads back together in the casserole, mix carefully to avoid breaking up the sweetbreads and serve. If you are of a whimsical turn of mind you can retrospectively torment any over-fastidious guests by not telling them what they are eating until after they have enjoyed it.

Number Twenty-Five – Three-and-a-Half-Bean Soup

*In which we attempt to throw some light on
the vexed question of portion size*

When we opened our hotel and restaurant in Buxton, we put this soup on our opening menu. The launch advertisement in the local paper was a simple one in which we printed the whole menu complete with prices, following the principle that the food would speak for itself. It's hard to credit it, but some weeks later the grapevine informed us with obvious relish that various Derbyshire worthies took the name of this soup as an indication of its quantity rather than its ingredients. Like a forest fire, the news had spread that our portions were weedy. We quickly learnt that, as Phineas Barnum was supposed to have observed, nobody ever went bust underestimating the intelligence of the public.

Due to the altitude, Buxton is cold and has a tendency to catch any rain or snow that's going. This also means that its occupants have a secret love affair with carbohydrate – Peak District restaurants tend to be assessed on the size of the chips they offer and little else is viewed as important. Against this backdrop it was foolhardy to make bad jokes about the ingredients of our soup.

Like so many things before it, this recipe owes a part of its inspiration to Chinese cuisine. The Chinese are great ones for assembling soups. You know the kind of thing: they take a highly flavoured clear stock and then float some nice dumplings in it; or some greens; or some noodles; or whatever. The result is a soup that stays clear, greens that stay crisp, tastes that complement one another rather than merging into a blur. It also tends to make for a very pretty bowlful. This soup starts with a good stock and then goes on to add three different coloured beans, and a third *half-bean* in the shape of sweetcorn. 'Three-and-a-half-bean soup' has another great plus point – by varying the ratio of stock to solids you can make it serve any purpose from looking elegant at the smarter dinner party to being the only dish of a filling supper.

This paragon amongst soups is also cheap and easy to prepare, although some would say a bit time-consuming. The initial building block is a strongly flavoured stock, and I have devoted some time to setting out a couple of examples.

INTRODUCTION

Concerning the beans: if you are starting from scratch you will have to be sure that the beans you need go through the lengthy ritual of soaking and thorough cooking – incorrectly cooked red beans can actually be poisonous. It's also sensible to wash all beans a couple of times in fresh water before and after soaking as this helps limit their combative effects on the digestion. Perhaps you'd rather circumvent this procedure by buying your beans ready-soaked and ready-cooked in tins from the supermarket. Your guests will be hard put to it to spot this short cut when they taste the end result.

INGREDIENTS FOR A CHICKEN STOCK

The carcass and trimmings of one or two chickens

2 large onions

2 leeks

2 carrots

2 sticks of celery

3 cloves of garlic

A good shake of dried oregano

A few whole black peppercorns

125 ml (4 fl oz) white wine

100 ml (3½ fl oz) white-wine vinegar

100 ml (3½ fl oz) good olive oil

INGREDIENTS FOR A RICH STOCK

1 pig's trotter

200 g (7 oz) shin of beef

2 large onions

2 leeks

2 carrots

2 sticks of celery

3 cloves of garlic

100 ml (3½ fl oz) good olive oil

2 good shakes of Worcestershire sauce

A few whole black peppercorns

125 ml (4 fl oz) red wine

100 ml (3½ fl oz) red-wine vinegar

METHOD FOR THE STOCKS

In each case the method is basically the same. Take all the ingredients on the list as far as garlic, and chop them coarsely; don't bother peeling the onions or carrots as their skins will help the colour of the finished stock; and remember that the trotter needs to be split lengthways so get your butcher to do that; put them into a roasting dish, splash the oil over them and give them forty minutes in a hot oven – gas mark 6 / 400°F / 200°C. Then transfer them to a large saucepan with the other ingredients, and just enough water barely to cover the surface, bring to the boil and turn down to a simmer. Leave for an hour. Strain through muslin into a bowl and leave to cool in the fridge. When cold remove the fat from the top, and if necessary reduce until you have about 1 litre (just under two pints) of liquid. If you prefer a stronger-tasting stock reduce it further. *Do not add any salt at any stage in the stock-making procedure.*

INGREDIENTS FOR THE SOUP

1.2 litres (2 pts) of stock

175 g (6 oz) of each of three different beans

175 g (6 oz) of cooked sweetcorn

1 bunch of spring onions chopped extremely finely

Decide on your beans, which must be pre-cooked. Pick a pleasing colour combination of three different sorts of bean from the following list (tinned beans come into their own here):

Haricot beans

Greek gigandes beans

Lima beans

Borlotti beans

Pinto beans

Flageolet beans

Black-eye beans

Crab-eye beans

Fejoiada – black beans

Red kidney beans

Cannellini beans

METHOD FOR THE SOUP

Heat the stock up and salt it to taste. Remember the solid qualities of the beans to be added and make it quite savoury. Add the chopped spring onions, add the beans, add the sweetcorn. Bring to the boil briefly and simmer for five minutes and serve, preferably in white bowls to set off the array of colours.

Number Twenty-Six – Orange Tenderloin

In which we consider improving the
National Curriculum

Wouldn't it be wonderful if every school-leaver went out into the world with a small portfolio of useful skills? Not mastery of trigonometry, Latin, physics and *The Anglo-Saxon Chronicle*, but something rather more sensible. Imagine what it would be like if everyone left school knowing how to swim; how to ride a bike; how to drive a car; how to fill in a tax form; how to type; how to take a shorthand note; how to cook a simple meal; how to speak a couple of European languages well enough to be understood; and how to get the best from a calculator or a computer?

I spent some formative years working in advertising in London. I was well paid, and to borrow one of Hugh, Lord Lonsdale's favourite sayings, 'Life was such lovely fun.' I was never burdened with quite such an onerous amount of money as he had, but I cannot remember ever being so well off. It's a great pity, but the race and pace of life in London means that the two prerequisites for comfortable living are youthful stamina and a corpulent wallet. Fortunately I was favoured with both, and whilst I've never mastered shorthand I could make a fair stab at cooking. I used to take a great pride in entertaining and from time to time would be approached by bachelor chums seeking inspiration. The requests were much the same, and ran along these lines: 'You do all that cooking stuff. What should I give so-and-so for dinner on Saturday; I thought I'd do a quiet dinner for just the two of us?'

Orange tenderloin was the dish I worked up as the centrepiece of my duffers' menu. Before it I would suggest Mermeesta, and afterwards fresh fruit salad. The whole meal worked on several levels: it was unlikely that the recipients would have tried any of the dishes before; nothing was very expensive; all the ingredients were readily available; and it was really difficult to make inedible through incompetence.

The first course was Mermeesta, a gallingly simple recipe that I stole from a friend, and able chef, Trevor Pharoah – chop up a hard-boiled egg and a couple of mushrooms, mix them with some cooked prawns in a fireproof dish (cocotte, or a mini-gratin dish), add salt, pepper and a sprinkle of mustard powder and moisten liberally with cream; pop into a hot oven for ten minutes and then add some grated Parmesan and breadcrumbs before returning to the oven to bake until the top is really crispy. Absolutely delicious and as easy as falling off a log. There was also the added plus of being able to invent elaborate and enthralling stories about the origins of the name 'Mermeesta' – my favourite was that the dish was originally of Dutch origin and something to do with the polders.

The fresh fruit salad was simply fresh fruit, peeled and prepared carefully, and then sloshed with Kirsch – in those faraway days this was daring but simple. The *pièce de résistance* was the orange tenderloin.

Orange tenderloin has stood the test of time because it presents the diner with easily eaten pieces of tender meat, looking attractive on a sauce that is strongly flavoured but not outlandish. It is simple and good, which is more than can be said for the motives of my bachelor friends who used to ask for the recipe.

INTRODUCTION

The first thing to be sure of is your pork. The exact bit of the animal is called the tenderloin, and in effect it is the piece of the porker which, if it were a bullock, would be called fillet steak. A long rope of meat with the grain running through it from end to end. Cunning butchers may try and make you use loin steaks, and various other appetisingly named bits and pieces, but you should really hold out for tenderloin, which to confuse matters further is sometimes also known as pork fillet. Get a whole one for a couple of diners: it will be about 25 cm (10 in) long and start at about 5 cm (2 in) across, tapering to a point. Trim away everything that looks even remotely unmeatlike – fat, membrane, untidy bits – and cut it across into eight perfect medallions 2 cm (1 in) thick. Keep what's left of the thinner, more pointy end for something else.

INGREDIENTS

Medallions of fresh pork tenderloin – 4 per person

75 g (2½ oz) unsalted butter

The juice of 6 freshly squeezed oranges

50 g (1½ oz) dark tangy marmalade

Salt and freshly ground black pepper

METHOD

Melt the butter in a frying pan and then cook the pork medallions in it over a low heat very slowly. As they begin to firm up take them out of the pan and put them to one side on a plate. Add the orange juice and the marmalade and cook fiercely until the sauce is nearly as thick as you would like it, season to taste with salt and a little pepper. Remember you need the contrast of the sweet/tart orange taste and the savoury flavour of salt; keep checking until it's just right. Then return the medallions to the pan and cook them briefly until they are done. Arrange four medallions on each plate and either strain the sauce on to them, or if you prefer splash it on – marmalade lumps, crispy bits and all. It depends how upmarket you want your dish to look. This dish benefits from some floury mashed potatoes to soak up the juice and perhaps a crisp green vegetable to give some colour contrast. It is surprising how good this tastes when you consider how easy it is to make.

Number Twenty-Seven – Stilton Sauce

In which we separate the warring factions in
Derbyshire, Nottinghamshire and Leicestershire

The first thing everyone has to get to grips with when talking about
Stilton cheese is that it doesn't come from the place of that name. In the
beginning, the cheese we now describe as Stilton was probably made by
a farmer's wife living in Woldenham called Mrs Paulet. Then in about
1790 that good lady's sister, a Mrs Thornhill, whose husband was
landlord of the Bell Inn at Stilton, turned this king amongst cheeses into
an eighteenth-century special offer for the London-bound coach passen-
gers, which resulted in the fame of Stilton cheese spreading like wildfire.
So that by the time Stilton gets a favourable mention in one of Jane
Austen's novels, and crops up a bit later in one of Charles Lamb's
famous letters, everyone seems to know just what it was they were
enthusing about.

Today Stilton comes from only five dairies in Derbyshire, Leicestershire and Nottinghamshire. The arguments over which cheese is the best
are violent, acrimonious, and have a longevity all of their own. That any
Stilton is made in the Peak District is merely a quirk of an earlier Duke of

Devonshire's penchant for fine cheese; the apocryphal tale has it that he so much enjoyed Stilton on a trip to Leicestershire that he bribed a local cheesemaker to move, with his herds and his workforce, to Derbyshire and set up a cheese-making operation in Hartington near Buxton. There matters rested for over a hundred years until cheese rivalry reared its head. Every year at food and wine events, whenever fine cheeses come under the critical eyes, and even more critical palates, of cheese luminaries, one or the other has to be chosen for the Stilton Cup.

In our time at the hotel, we were fortunate enough to have Richard Davies from the dairy in nearby Hartington – a notable Stilton maker – as a speaker at one of the Gastronomes' dinners. The menu we offered featured, and complemented, various local cheeses and read as follows:

Menu for the fifth meeting of the Buxton Gastronomes
at Cold Springs House Hotel

THE BEST OF BRITISH BLUE CHEESES
Speaker – Richard Davies

Salad of pousse épinards with mâche and oak leaf lettuces,
smoked bacon pieces and a Buxton Blue dressing

Mignons of fillet of beef with a Stilton sauce,
new potatoes and fresh vegetables

A raspberry sorbet

A cheeseboard comprising:
young Stilton, mature Stilton and white Stilton,
Buxton Blue and blue Wensleydale
to illustrate Richard's talk

Coffee

I have to confess that aside from some glorious cheeses, at that fleeting point of perfect ripeness, and the excellence of Richard's informative and entertaining talk, the only notable feature of the dinner was the Stilton sauce, and like so many nice dishes it was relatively straightforward to make. Stilton has such a sledgehammer flavour, strong and almost salty, that the chef's primary task is to let all that flavour bask in its own glory.

When you taste a great piece of Stilton you can see why some gourmets recommend enjoying it with a glass of dessert wine, an old oloroso or a decent Australian liqueur muscat.

You can also understand why Roger Verge of the Moulin de Mougins described it as 'Un veritable delice'. All in all, it was touch-and-go deciding whether to include this recipe for Stilton sauce as it is probably sacrilege to use such a cheese for cooking with. On the other hand the sauce does taste very good indeed.

INTRODUCTION

This sauce is robust and fully flavoured and so it is best used with beef or venison, meats with enough about them to 'fight back', or at the other extreme over plain pasta, or perhaps a baked potato when you can enjoy the flavour alone in its glory. You need Stilton of course, and in common with most things the general principle that the better the quality of the ingredients you start with, then the better will be your finished dish, holds good.

At this point it is hard to resist a short detour into the 'How to serve Stilton' controversy. It seems to me that the dig-in-with-a-spoon-and-add-glass-of-port school have been badly misled. This is a quick and easy way to spoil not only the cheese but the port as well. Treat Stilton like any other fine cheese: not too much fridge, cut off what you need as you need it, and don't sweat it in a plastic bag. I must confess that in these guidelines I am only reaffirming the excellent advice offered by the Stilton Cheesemakers' Association.

INGREDIENTS

25 g (1 oz) white, plain flour

50 g (2 oz) good unsalted butter

500 ml (18 fl oz) whole milk

Salt, freshly ground black pepper, ground mace

125 g (4½ oz) ripe Stilton

50 ml (2 fl oz) double cream

METHOD

There is no substitute for practice. This Stilton sauce is basically a béchamel sauce with knobs on, and like all sauces the béchamel can end up as thick as porridge or as thin as milk. It's really up to you to decide how you like it; have a trial run and see for yourself. If you follow the quantities given here slavishly, you will strike what I believe is a happy medium, but were I in your place, I would not hesitate to add in a bit more flour or a bit more butter if I felt that was the right thing to do. You shouldn't hesitate to do so either.

So, to work – melt the butter gently in a frying pan, and whilst that is happening put the milk on to a medium heat in another pan with a good pinch of ground mace. Add the flour to the frying pan and cook the resulting roux gently, don't brown it too much (a purely cosmetic consideration). Do cook the roux thoroughly, and then when the milk has come to the boil add about a quarter of it to the frying pan and work it in carefully. The way that the milk and roux merge into one is fascinating to watch, but you must keep stirring, then add the next quarter of a pint of milk, stir, cook, and repeat until you have amalgamated all the flour and all the milk. And no, this procedure will not work just as well with cold milk! It is important to cook the flour thoroughly and so avoid the nasty metallic taste that could otherwise pose a problem. Then take the Stilton and crumble it into the béchamel, stirring as it dissolves, preferably with a balloon whisk. Do not let the sauce boil once you have added the cheese. Taste the sauce and adjust the seasoning with salt and pepper to taste. Finally beat in the cream to *polish* the sauce. Check seasoning once more. Serve and collect the compliments.

Number Twenty-Eight – Chicken Liver Bolognaise

*In which we contrive to make healthy
eating a tad jollier*

It's not much of an exaggeration to say that I enjoyed my first spaghetti Bolognaise 'at my mother's knee'. And if this revelation conjures up mental pictures of a bustling Italian family, with plenty of aunts in black shawls and a backing track consisting of Caruso played scratchily at 78 rpm, then I'm sorry to disappoint you. In real life the cast was largely Anglo-Saxon and the setting was the roomy kitchen of a large creaky house in Leamington Spa. What was truly remarkable was the kind of Bolognaise sauce we were enjoying, and the fact that we were enjoying it before the recent rebirth of Italian food in Britain.

You see, my mother's spag Bol recipe made use of all manner of daring continental ingredients – tomato purée, chicken livers, wine, even olive oil and garlic. Nowadays, it is hard to understand just how adventurous this all was, but by way of explanation, throughout most of Britain chicken livers were once popular as a cheap food for the cat; wine meant Mateus Rosé or Blue Nun; garlic's only role was as a vital prop in horror films; and olive oil was something you bought in tiny bottles from the chemist when you needed to dislodge wax from your ears.

So you can tell that I was subverted by good food at an early age. Since then there have been so many changes, fads have come and also gone, and good food has achieved some status of its own. Anyway, prey as we are to all these changing influences, everybody I know goes through phases when 'healthy eating' seems the one true path, and it was in just such a mood that I developed this recipe. One of the great revelations of an expanding knowledge of food and diet was that pasta was a complex carbohydrate and as such could be good for you. For slaves to the calorie counter this was exceedingly good news indeed.

But there were other great revelations too: extra virgin olive oil was high in mono-unsaturates, and garlic was good for your blood, and we always knew that liver was good for you.

If the contents of the average store cupboard changes rapidly, it's a slowcoach compared with pasta. From strands of iron-hard spaghetti, which used to be sold in long folds of thick blue paper so that it looked like a deadly firework, there has been an explosion of different types, styles and shapes of pasta. I'm not suggesting that you limit this dish to rare squid ink pasta or anything so exotic, but I do urge you to try it with a different shape – but buy good quality dried pasta.

INTRODUCTION

This recipe is set out in quantities that are sufficient to feed four. You'll have to scale it up or down as you see fit. As to the ingredients, any pasta will do whether it is in ribbons, spirals, yellow, green or red! To add weight to the healthy eating argument, I have also made a rough calculation of the calories involved in cooking this dish (see the ingredients section). Of course this is only a general guide and anything more accurate you'll have to work out from the particular brands you use when you make the dish yourself. It is generally encouraging, however, to think that a portion of this magnificent dish is likely to have only a third the calories of a fish-and-chip supper; to be low in saturated fat and high in polyunsaturated fats; and to contain a beneficial amount of iron. In addition it will prove cheap to make and delicious to eat.

INGREDIENTS

150 g (5½ oz) fresh or frozen chicken livers	205 kcal
175 g (6 oz) strong onions	40 kcal
175 g (6 oz) celery	12 kcal
175 g (6 oz) grated carrot	20 kcal
3 cloves of fresh garlic	10 kcal
400 g tin of chopped tomatoes, typically,	100 kcal
A good dash of Worcestershire sauce	10 kcal
100 ml (3½ fl oz) red wine, typically,	70 kcal

50 ml (2 fl oz) good olive oil   530 kcal

500 g pack of pasta, typically   1350 kcal

a total of 2347 kcal

That works out at under 600 kcal per head, which is not bad for a break out that tastes as good as this one.

METHOD

Start at least forty minutes before you want to eat. Or even better make the sauce a day ahead and keep it covered in the fridge until you need it. Chop the onions and celery finely and cook them slowly in the olive oil in a large frying pan. Crush the garlic into the pan and add the carrots, and continue to cook slowly. Your objective is to get as much water out of the vegetables as you can without caramelising the sugar in the onions (i.e. before they turn brown).

Chop the chicken livers and add them to the mix, cook them through. Then add the wine, Worcestershire sauce and the tin of tomatoes and stir well. Turn the heat up full and continue stirring. As the sauce boils, the alcohol will be driven out of the wine and the sauce will lose water (there's lots in the tinned tomatoes) and thicken up. Stop this procedure when the sauce has reached the consistency you would wish your spaghetti sauce to be. Turn the heat off and leave the sauce for the flavours to blend. If you want to leave the sauce sitting there for two or three hours it doesn't matter. Just before you want to eat, cook the pasta. Follow the instructions on the packet – it should take no more than four or five minutes. Then drain it. Heat your sauce through and amalgamate the two halves of this dish. Put on your *Godfather* sound-track CD and enjoy. This will be nearly as enjoyable as the smugness you will derive from knowing that you have strayed by as little as 600 kcal.

Number Twenty-Nine – Auntie Lena's Ginger Biscuits

In which we reflect on the role of ginger
in matters equestrian

During my incarnation as an ad man, one of the most elaborate commercials I ever wrote was cancelled two days before shooting was due to start. At that point we had recorded the music; cast the stars; and a backlot at Shepperton Studios had been remade as a Caribbean paradise; and we'd even had a pit dug to get the camera down really low. The ruination of our plans was an activist called Michael Manley and a 'little local difficulty' in Jamaica. The Jamaicans had decided to let the ginger crop rot in the ground as some kind of political gesture, and my musical epic, featuring as it did a friendly Jamaican ginger grower and his search for perfect ginger and the perfect ginger biscuit, was mortally wounded. Jamaica's withdrawal from the market meant that the biscuit factory was forced to find another source for its ginger supplies, and after many trials and tribulations another supplier was found . . . in Nigeria. The only slight problem was that friendly Nigerian ginger growers don't calypso about a Shepperton set making the public feel good about biscuits half as authentically as the Jamaican ginger growers the public has come to know and love. My commercial was doomed before the cameras had even turned over.

Ginger is wonderful stuff: it can add heat and pizazz to drinks, starters, meat, fish, puddings; and, as was well known to the shadier members of the horse-dealing fraternity, horses. The phrase 'to ginger something up' is supposed to have been derived from the practice of putting a spring into the step of a particularly elderly and infirm nag by the eye-watering expedient of lifting its tail and inserting a length of peeled root ginger. 'Auntie Lena's ginger biscuits' give you that bit of extra snap that you just don't get from shop-bought biscuits, in a slightly less traumatic fashion. I am proud to claim that I am related to the Auntie Lena, but only by marriage. Auntie Lena is my mother-in-law's aunt (or my wife's great-aunt if that seems more succinct). I stole the recipe for her justly famed ginger biscuits from my mother-in-law's recipe notebook where it had been a closely guarded secret for a great many years. As soon as I tried this recipe out, I knew that it was a winner.

You can make these biscuits in two styles, and they always seem to work. Either roll them out on the thick side so that the finished biscuits are crunchy outside but fairly chewy inside, or roll them out as thin as you dare and have them crisp as shrapnel. In my search for complete authenticity, I baked a batch in each style and tried them out on the mother-in-law. 'Which way,' I asked her, 'did Auntie Lena bake them, crisp or chewy?' 'Both ways,' she replied.

So there you have it. A delicious, dual-purpose biscuit that's easy to make and a delight to eat. When it's on the thick side then it has a chewy middle and just begs to be dunked in a cup of tea, and when it's thin it has an almost brandy-snap quality to it that means you need not be ashamed to serve it with an ice cream or bavarois.

INTRODUCTION

When you first read this recipe, your first thought will probably be that it is never going to work. As you glance through the ingredients you'll be brought up short by the extremely small amount of liquid in the mixture. 'Ahem,' you will say to yourself, 'this will be the very devil to roll out.' Well, take heart, it's not child's play but it is pretty easy, and it does work every time. The only change I have made from the original is to make the *greedy man's choice* and use butter instead of margarine, and to cut back a little on the amount of sugar involved.

INGREDIENTS

40 g (1½ oz) unsalted butter

225 g (8 oz) plain flour

175 g (6 oz) caster sugar

1 good tbs golden syrup

1 good tsp ground ginger

1 tsp salt

½ tsp bicarbonate of soda dissolved in a tablespoonful of
warm water seconds before you need to add it to the mix

METHOD

Take a large mixing bowl, and mix the flour, sugar, ginger and salt. Then rub in the butter. Add the golden syrup and then the bicarbonate of soda, which you have just dissolved in a tablespoonful of warm water. Mix thoroughly without adding any more liquid, and you will be amazed to see that soon it changes to a pliable dough you can roll out. Cut out your biscuits, choosing to make them as thick or as thin as your mood dictates. Put them on a baking sheet covered with a sheet of silicone baking parchment and bake them in a pre-heated oven, gas between mark 2 & 3 / 310°F / 155°C. Take a look at the biscuits after twenty minutes. Obviously just when they are done will depend on precisely how thinly you have rolled them out. The key to success is to inspect them fairly frequently and trust to your intuition. Cool them on a rack and then, as another old family recipe puts it, 'These will keep for several days in a tin inside a well-locked cupboard.'

Number Thirty – Rabbit with Prunes

In which we side with Mr McGregor
rather than Benjamin

Throughout children's literature bunny rabbits have been let off unusually lightly. I don't recall any sympathy for Mr McGregor. If Brer Rabbit had been eaten not briar patched, we'd have saved ourselves a good deal of moralising. As is so often the case, only Mole in *Wind in the Willows* shows any kind of good sense as he rushes to the riverbank, bowling stout rabbits out of his path whilst mocking them with sly asides of 'Onion sauce! Onion sauce!'

There was a time when all the sympathy was on the side of the rabbit. Myxomatosis was a shocking and artificially introduced disease that left dying and blinded rabbits crawling about the countryside and mankind with an unfortunate burden of blame to bear. No one, but no one, fancied eating a wild rabbit then. But before the Second World War most country families had rabbit once a week and no wonder: it was cheap, tasty and good for you.

In the older editions of Mrs Beeton (revised at the beginning of the 1960s) there are half a dozen rabbit recipes, plus instruction on drawing and skinning; in *Farmhouse Fare* (recipes gathered just before the Second World War) there's a whole section. But when you come to *bibles* like Delia Smith's *Complete Cookery Course* there's only a single rabbit recipe. On the Continent rabbit, as an ingredient, has weathered the storm a bit better, probably because farmed rabbits are more readily available. This should be the age of the great UK rabbit comeback. Just after one Christmas our local butcher in Worcester had seventy wild rabbits hung up in the shop. They had been caught by ferreting so there was no lead shot to break your teeth on. Each rabbit provided a couple of pounds of lean meat; low in cholesterol; with no hormonal growth promoters. And at a cost that made them half the price per pound of supermarket sausages. Rabbits represent an amazing bargain, as well as being really healthy eating.

This dish of rabbit with prunes has been designed to compensate for the only slight disadvantage of rabbit meat – because it is so lean it can prove dry. When Mrs Beeton recommended roast rabbit she did so to a hardier and less discerning population.

For this reason rabbit with prunes is a two-stage dish, and the unctuous gravy is made on day one, using a variety of cheap bits and pieces which you will be able to acquire from the butcher where you find your rabbit (if no tame butcher springs to mind immediately, try any of the larger supermarkets). In the introduction, I also suggest a jointing method that's not wildly wasteful, but does make the finished dish a bit easier to eat.

It just remains for you to find a way of convincing the younger members of your family that it is not the Flopsy Bunnies who are to be found reclining in your favourite casserole dish.

INTRODUCTION

Bones. Bones are what tend to put so many people off rabbit. Ask your butcher for the rabbit whole and then cut it up yourself. This is a good deal easier than it at first appears. Lay the rabbit on its back and pretend that it is a chicken. Take the back legs off the whole just as you would remove the thigh and drumstick of a chicken. Then take the front legs off as if they were its wings – just cut them off at the joint that is nearest to the body. You are left with the body – cut it in half just behind the shortest rib. Keep the back bit, which is known as the saddle, and put the other bit which involves the rib cage, liver, etc., to one side. If you start off with two rabbits your casserole will end up with six excellent bits of meat (two saddles and four back legs) and four that are all right (the four front legs). This is plenty for four hungry diners.

As for the other element in the dish, the prunes, those no-need-to-soak-ready-stoned prunes are absolutely wonderful.

INGREDIENTS FOR THE STOCK

The rib cage sections of 2 fresh, young, wild rabbits, which
you saved when you jointed the rabbits – as we discussed
in the introduction

1 whole pig's trotter – ask your butcher to split it lengthwise
with a cleaver

225 g (8 oz) shin of beef

2 whole medium onions

2 sticks of celery

3 cloves of garlic

1 large carrot

125 ml (4 fl oz) red wine

50 ml (2 fl oz) red-wine vinegar

A good shake of Worcestershire sauce

1 tsp dried thyme

A sprinkling of whole black peppercorns

1 tbs virgin olive oil

INGREDIENTS FOR THE MAIN DISH

The stock as prepared

2 medium onions, peeled and finely chopped

1 tbs good olive oil

The ten rabbit joints

175 g (6 oz) ready to eat, pitted prunes
Salt and freshly ground black pepper

METHOD

Day One – the stock.

Joint the rabbits as outlined in the introduction. Put the 'best bits' into the fridge and get out your largest roasting dish. Put the rib cages into it. Chop the shin of beef into chunks and add them. Add the pig's trotter. Cut the onions into quarters (skin and all – the skin will add colour to the final dish) and pop them in. Split the carrot into quarters lengthwise and add it. Add the celery cut into manageable lengths. Cut the garlic cloves across – again unpeeled – and add them. Roast the whole lot in a hot oven – gas mark 7 / 425°F / 220°C – for forty minutes. Then transfer to your stockpot and add the liquids and herbs, finally adding enough water to cover everything by about 3 cm (1 in). Bring to the boil and then simmer for two hours, topping up from time to time with boiling water. Then strain off through a very fine sieve or, preferably, doubled muslin. Return to a shallow pan and reduce fiercely until you have 500 ml (18 fl oz) of liquid left. Cool in a bowl or jug and leave in the fridge overnight.

Congratulations, you have accomplished the hard part.

Day Two – the main event.

Seal your rabbit joints in a frying pan using some of the olive oil. Then use the rest of the oil to fry the chopped onions until they are transparent. Arrange the fried onions and the rabbit joints in your favourite casserole. Then take your bowl of jellied stock from the fridge, discard the scum and fat that has congealed on the surface and add the rich jelly to the casserole. Put it in a moderate oven – gas mark 4 / 350°F / 180°C – for two hours. After two hours, which should be half an hour before you want to serve the dish, take the casserole out of the oven, strain off all the gravy into a saucepan, add the prunes to the pot and return it to a slow oven – gas mark 2 / 300°F / 150°C – to keep hot. Now you can work on the sauce. First reduce it until it is as thick and syrupy as you like it. (Or you may wish to thicken it at this juncture with a little potato flour or cornflour.) Then add salt and ground black pepper to taste.

All that remains is to recombine the sauce and the rabbit joints and serve.

Number Thirty-One – Red Devil

In which we envy the lot of
French lorry drivers

We were on our way to the England versus France rugby International at the Parc des Princes, and rather astutely my three companions and I had allowed ourselves a week in Burgundy beforehand, as a kind of *warm-up*. Our holiday was not without incident. Travelling as we were – four prop forwards shoehorned into a smallish French hire car – a quiet and uneventful time would have been a disappointment.

Gastronomically speaking, we hoped to peak midweek at the restaurant Côte d'Or in Nuits St Georges which had, at that time, a strong two stars in the Michelin guide. We stayed opposite in the Hôtel des Cultivateurs, which was a splendid and unpretentious hostelry. The dinner was magnificent, it cost half a king's ransom and was worth every penny. As we walked back over the road we speculated amongst ourselves as to whether there was any better meal to be had in France, Europe, or indeed the universe.

The next morning dawned, and with it the tiniest twinge of headache. I walked into town where it was complemented by one of the most savage haircuts it has ever been my pleasure to brag about. The day lay before us and we decided to drive off in a north-westerly direction and take a look around. Little did we know as we decided against breakfast that we were merely leaving room for what was undoubtedly the finest lunch in the universe.

By the morning's end we had ventured up to Châteauneuf en Auxerre, and were casually following the Burgundian canal when our finely tuned digestions signalled lunchtime. Coming through the next village we spotted a flock of lorries parked in an otherwise unprepossessing side street, at which point a gentleman in *bleu de travail*, complete with Gauloise and beret, came out of a plain door looking smug. Over his shoulder we could see rows of similarly dressed gents sitting down to an excellent lunch. We parked the car and went in.

Inside were two rooms, each with a large table. In one, the serried ranks of diners looked up and wished us 'bonjour'. We were ushered into the other which was graced with a fine old linen press. It was time for the bold decision, so when the fierce-looking, black-garbed lady asked, 'Menu?' we replied, 'Menu!'

We had committed ourselves to the standard fare and were in for the best meal in the universe. Granny appeared from the kitchen to inspect us. There was much murmuring of 'Les Anglais'. Bread was forthcoming, four glasses, and from under the table a litre bottle of splendid, fresh red wine with plastic push-off cap.

The first course arrived – a platter of thinly sliced dried ham, cornichons and grated celeriac in a simple dressing. There was silence from our party as each attended to the inner man. Then came the second salvo – a thick steak of freshly poached salmon sitting on a sharp sorrel sauce. Strangely enough the cool red wine seemed to go well with the fish, and when we asked for another bottle we were told to help ourselves from the serried ranks under the table. Then followed a coq-au-vin with whisper-crisp allumette potatoes. Then an amazing pot of home-made *fromage fort* which, after I had gathered my shocked wits and blitzkrieged tongue, was later to become my inspiration for 'Red Devil'. *Fromage fort* is essentially potted cheese, but it's angrier, stronger and far more virulent than anything the British Isles can boast. Sometimes it is rolled into little cones and dusted with cayenne pepper to make *boulette*.

Afterwards, with our tastebuds in tatters, there was a soothing slice of ice cream and a cup of coffee. This meal was an epic, full of genuine flavours, contrast and care. In every way the equal of the night before's extravagance except in one respect, the price! Our lunch had cost one tenth of the dinner in Nuits St Georges. To put that into even sharper perspective, a five-course lunch with unlimited wine had cost us roughly what we would have paid for two pints of bitter beer and a ham sandwich at home in London.

No wonder everybody, but everybody, goes out to lunch every day in

France. If that kind of value could be found over here, no doubt the British would too. However, *fromage fort* and 'Red Devil' would never be more than a minority delicacy – a cruel spur to a jaded palate. Consider the implications: you only start to make 'Red Devil' when the cheese concerned has gone so far past its best that it is verging on the inedible.

You have been warned!

INTRODUCTION

This is a practical dish made from leftovers. I find it works best with geriatric Stilton and a bit of Cheddar. But all kinds of variations are permitted. The guiding principle is that you need roughly three parts smelly cheese, to one part bulk cheese. On the vexed question as to whether you should include the rind; that tends to depend upon the rind – if it is armour plate, or waxed, or impossibly gnarled, then no; if otherwise, why not? In a similar vein, I use a drop of malt whisky to help the dish on its way, but brandy, or even at a pinch sherry, will do as well, and omitting alcohol entirely is no sin either.

INGREDIENTS

350 g (12 oz) rank and smelly cheese
150 g (5½ oz) milder, firmer cheese
30 ml (1 fl oz) malt whisky
A good dash of Worcestershire sauce

125 g (4½ oz) butter – clarified

1 tsp sweet red paprika

1 tsp red cayenne pepper

½ tsp salt

125 g (4½ oz) further melted, unsalted butter to seal the pots

METHOD

Take all the ingredients and blend, or pound in a mortar, until they are a homogeneous paste. Pack your 'Red Devil' into ramekins or small pots (these quantities will be right for four). Run a 5 mm (½ in) skim of melted clarified butter over the top to seal, and store in the fridge. When it has set, inspect your pots for irritating cracks or fissures in the butter that would hinder keeping, and if necessary add another layer of clarified butter. Keep 'Red Devil' for at least a week to mature, and eat carefully and with great respect – these are flavours that take no prisoners.

Number Thirty-Two – Smart-Looking Salmon

*In which we marvel at the creativity of
fishmongers in general*

Salmon just isn't what it was. And I'm not harking back to the oft-
quoted instance when the apprentices of London had it written into
their articles that they shouldn't be forced to eat salmon more than
three times a week.

Once there was a glut of salmon in Britain, then there was none, and
now once again there is a glut. But it still lingers in everyone's mind that
salmon is a luxury. So much so, that whenever you set up a buffet with
a whole cold salmon as centrepiece it's invariably the salmon that looks
as if it might run out. It is strangely difficult to overestimate people's
appetite for fresh salmon.

And very nice salmon is too, with one reservation. Once you have
tasted that great rarity, a genuinely wild, sea-fresh salmon that's merely
been poached in *court bouillon* and brought to the table when quite cold
with a newly baked loaf and a bowl of thick mayonnaise made with some
fresh tarragon and a decent olive oil, most other salmon dishes will lose
their charm. But such is the environmental pressure the Atlantic salmon

is under, unless you know an able fisherman with a plump wallet or Debrett relatives, you're very unlikely to get genuine wild, genuinely fresh salmon unless you put your own chequebook at the mercy of either a top-flight fishmonger or a professional poacher.

You'll get wild/farmed salmon (fish which have been roaming a fairly large area of sea whilst being fed to size); a 'farmed' salmon (fish kept in a cramped saltwater cage and fed pellets, the equivalent in both animal and gastronomic terms of the battery hen); or a wild salmon caught at sea by a Norwegian boat and frozen or iced down for its voyage to you along the distribution chain – at least the latter has eaten wild food, but this is reflected in a high price.

As for the fish called sewin, peal, or sea trout – it tastes so delicate and wonderful that it would make you give up wild salmon – but you're unlikely ever to get one of those unless you catch it yourself, or have good contacts at weekly markets in Wales. Unscrupulous fishmongers will try and sell you sea trout – by which they mean freshwater rainbow trout that have been imprisoned in a salt water cage. My advice is don't bother unless you can catch one yourself.

When buying salmon, accept the limitations of the marketplace and look for fish that are still firm, that don't smell (watch out in particular for a faint hint of ammonia), and that don't look too ragged about the fins. Then buy one, and turn it into a smart-looking salmon. This recipe came about when technology stepped in and made a giant contribution to the presentation of the dish. That was the moment when I found out about steaming things in little parcels. *En papillote* is the best thing that ever happened to steaming. You wrap the food with an airtight seal, so the food cooks in its own steam; it keeps many layered foods wrapped tightly together; and the end results are easy to serve – simply cut open the tinfoil envelope with a pair of scissors and hey presto. In this dish we wrap the piece of salmon fillet in a dark green leaf to make a clean-cut rectangular parcel, then wrap it in a snug-fitting aluminium foil envelope and turn the joins over themselves a couple of times to ensure a good seal. When you unveil it, the green brick of salmon looks superb sitting on a sea of deep yellow sauce (a *beurre blanc* is ideal) or a simple white and green sorrel sauce. Then when you cut into the parcel there is yet another pleasing contrast – the pink of the fish against the green of the leaves.

And remember, long before we taste anything, we have already eaten it with our eyes.

INTRODUCTION

Having already discussed what kind of salmon you are seeking to buy, it's probably as well to devote some time to just how to prepare it. If you have a good fishmonger he can be counted on to carry out any or all of these procedures; if not then buy a whole gutted fish and do it yourself. It really isn't that difficult.

Take your salmon and fillet it. You need to arrive at two long pieces (which you keep) and a head, tail and backbone (which goes for stock). Cut the head off and work towards the tail, lifting the flesh away from the backbone one side at a time. Take each fillet and trim off the gnarled bits where the fins were; go over the plump side of the flesh and pull out any remaining small bones that protrude (they're called the pin bones). A pair of long-nosed pliers kept for the purpose is a godsend, and will also prove useful for other fiddly kitchen jobs (keyless sardine tins; broken champagne wires). Eventually you should have two long fillets of salmon – skin one side, flesh the other, and no bones. Lay each down on a board, skin side down, and with a long sharp knife push down and along between the skin and the flesh in a kind of scraping movement and you'll find that by keeping up the downward pressure as you run the knife along, you can lift the flesh off the skin fairly easily. Then you are left with two salmon fillets, no skin, no bones. Simply cut them across into portions.

INGREDIENTS FOR THE SALMON

Sufficient pieces of salmon fillet for your guests

A large bunch of sorrel, or of spinach, or perhaps a savoy
    cabbage, or a large cos lettuce

50 g (1½ oz) melted, unsalted butter

METHOD FOR THE SALMON

First get your steamer going. The bamboo ones from Chinese super-markets do an excellent job at a fraction the price of the stainless steel ones from cookshops.

First take your green leaves and wilt them in boiling water immediately before plunging them into cold water to refresh them. Take each salmon steak and brush it with some melted butter, salt it and pepper it, and then wrap it neatly in the green leaves without too many overlaps, making sure the joints are on the bottom.

Then brush a sheet of tinfoil with butter and put the fish parcel on to it. Then the tinfoil needs to be done up so that it holds the package together gently, and sealed so that it is airtight. Then steam the packets; you will be surprised by how quickly they cook. Seven or eight minutes should be enough for all but the largest piece of fish. It is easy to tell when they are done; simply take each packet out and press down on it. With a little practice you will soon learn the degree of firmness that shows the fish is cooked. Then serve by cutting open the foil and presenting the dark-green rectangle on a sea of *beurre blanc*.

INGREDIENTS FOR THE BEURRE BLANC

100 g (3½ oz) finely chopped shallots

80 ml (3 fl oz) good white-wine vinegar

80 ml (3 fl oz) water

250 g pack unsalted butter

Salt and freshly ground black pepper

METHOD FOR THE BEURRE BLANC

Cook the finely chopped shallots gently in the vinegar and water. After about ten minutes you will notice that the mixture has reduced to a small quantity with a jam-like consistency. Take a balloon whisk and your butter, which should be at room temperature and cut into little chunks, turn up the heat, and use the whisk to work the butter into the shallot mixture to make a smooth sauce. When all the butter is safely incorporated, season with salt and pepper and strain to remove the shallot pieces. Serve the salmon sitting atop a pool of this rich yellow sauce. You'll be well on your way to finding out that this salmon recipe is not only smart-looking but smart-tasting as well.

Number Thirty-Three – Banana Tea Bread

In which we address the question,
'When is a cup not a cup?'

In the days before central heating, double glazing and loft insulation, afternoon tea represented an important refuelling stop on the journey through the day. Cold meats, biscuits and iced fancies were all very well but the serious work of the tea table revolved around buns and breads.

The sternest tea I ever faced was at Crail on the Fife coast. I had accompanied some friends from St Andrews University, where they were committed to a winter term of *Childe Harold* and a dark fizzy beer called 'heavy' that claimed the lion's share of their attention. Scotland was enduring that combination of the grey and dank weather the Scots call 'dreekit', and regular power cuts. The cottage that did the teas was small and dark, and with the power suspended, the only light sources were an open fire – which was also pressed into service for toasting things and boiling water – and a couple of flickering oil lamps. It was a simple matter to imagine just what life must have been like in the last century. Tea started with some bread and butter, moved to a pair of oak-smoked kippers or some 'finny haddocks', flirted with some scones, reprised the bread and butter with jam, introduced a towering, butter-dripping stack of crumpets, and reached a triumphant crescendo with a majestic forward line of cakes. But these were not the elegant little cakes of southern climes, these were solid, fruit-speckled, blocks of cake.

Nowadays, sedentary and pampered as we are, we don't crave carbohydrate quite so much and in consequence we should look at the older tea bread and cake recipes carefully to see just what we want from them. In a roundabout sort of way this is just what my wife achieved when she first tried what has since become a family favourite: this recipe for banana tea bread. Once again this is one of those delightful but infuriating old-fashioned recipes that talks airily of taking a cup of this and four ounces of that and so forth. In common with the rest of us, Sylvia was faced with choosing one of the kitchen mugs or a coffee cup to measure with and she chose a coffee cup. And that's where fate took a hand because the cup she decided on was on the small side. (For the record a British Standard measuring cup has a capacity of 10 fluid ounces, as does a breakfast cup; a tea cup, however, holds 6⅔ fluid ounces; and an American and Canadian standard measuring cup holds 8 fluid ounces). In effect what my wife had achieved was to reduce the amount of sugar and flour in the recipe but retain the full quota of bananas. And as a principle for adapting the rather stodgy recipes from chillier times it works very well.

This new slant radically alters the texture of the finished product. It gets a lot wetter. A lot more squidgy. A lot less like bread. And a lot tastier. Why do cakes have to be dry and airy? Why not something more self-indulgent, and more along the lines of the American fudge brownie? Moist. Moreish. The kind of cake that would stick to the wall if thrown.

If you're looking for a cake that genuinely tastes of bananas and is satisfyingly soggy inside but has a nice brown crust outside – search no farther.

INTRODUCTION

Generally speaking, cakes are leavened either by biological or chemical means. This recipe relies on the latter, and in its original form not only used self-raising flour but also a sour milk and bicarbonate of soda mixture (so that the acid of the milk would react with the bicarb to produce CO_2). As we are trying for a closer textured, moister cake this recipe uses fresh milk and omits the extra bicarb.

This is a great way of using up those very ripe bananas that have been languishing at the rear of the fruit bowl for some days too long. You know the ones, the ones with an outside that has turned black and an inside that has an almost unbearable honeyed sweetness.

INGREDIENTS

175 g (6 oz) caster sugar

225 g (8 oz) white self-raising flour

100 g (3½ oz) unsalted butter

3 tbs fresh milk

2 large fresh eggs

3 medium sized, very ripe bananas

A few drops of vanilla essence

METHOD

You have two options, either you can use a food processor, which will result in a finer and more homogeneous texture, or you can do it the traditional way which leaves larger – almost recognisable – bits of banana in the finished cake. Personally (and because I have a fondness for really soggy cake), I am wedded to the food processor. Traditionally speaking you should cream the fat with the sugar and then add the eggs, milk and the mashed bananas, before finally working in the flour. With a food processor, simply whizz everything together until you have a smooth batter. Then take an ordinary large loaf tin and butter it well, paying particular attention to the cracks and corners. Put a little flour into it and tap the tin to distribute it evenly and then empty it out to leave a miserly coating. If you have a belt and braces side to your cookery it doesn't hurt to line the floor of the tin with baking parchment as well. Put the mixture into the prepared tin and bake.

The oven setting should be – gas between mark 4 & 5 / 360°F / 185°C. Check after the cake has been in an hour, it'll probably be done. Because we are looking for a soggy end product, the old-faithful test of sticking in a skewer and withdrawing it clean is not appropriate. With practice you'll simply need to glance at it to tell. In the meantime, because of the style of cake we're trying to achieve, there's a wide margin of error to make things easier. This banana tea bread makes a delicious change, even if you don't feel the need to enjoy a couple of kippers before moving on to it!

Number Thirty-Four – Herb Oil

In which we range freely from
Scandinavia to Mediterranean shores

One of my advertising colleagues had a pet theory that the peoples of Europe – and their buying preferences – could be divided into three sectors on the basis of two key indicators.

In the North – from the Arctic to the north of England – they were 'spirit to drink and lard to cook with'. In the middle part – from the north of England down as far as the middle of France – they were 'beer to drink and butter to cook with'. And in the southern part – from the middle of France down to the Mediterranean – they were 'wine to drink and oil to cook with'. It's a pleasing theory that tallies superficially with morose Scandinavians and Scots slugging aquavit and whisky whilst frying things in lard; plump Englishmen, Germans and Belgians quaffing beer and spreading butter thickly; and laid-back Frenchmen, Italians and Spaniards sunning themselves whilst drinking wine, covering everything in olive oil.

It's also pleasing to see UK opinion 'drifting south' on this scale in response to the relentless pressure from dietitians, doctors and other opinionated medical worthies. As a consequence, using olive oil has become *de rigeur*, butter has become an indulgence, and lard something unspeakable. At least this change in the dynamics of the market has brought down the price of good quality olive oil.

And where the olive leads, many others follow. At the last count you could try walnut oil, hazelnut oil, avocado oil, argan oil, almond oil, pistachio oil, pinenut oil, groundnut oil, grape pip oil, corn oil, canola oil, palm oil, sesame oil, sunflower oil, pumpkin-seed oil and probably a good many more that don't immediately spring to mind. I have to say that after an initial mad dash trying them all I've settled down, and now we keep just a good olive oil, some walnut oil, some hazelnut oil, and some sesame oil particularly for Chinese cooking. This spartan approach means that every time a recipe calls for oil, it gets virgin olive oil.

So when we received a bottle of home-made herb oil for Christmas one year it was a most welcome addition to our armoury, and prompted me to look into recipes for herb oils. They fall into two main categories: there are oils that taste strongly of herbs, where the taste of the oil is merely a backdrop to the predominant flavour of the herb concerned; and there are strong oils with an additional flavouring of some kind, such as a heavy olive oil with a touch of garlic.

Both are equally useful about the kitchen, and in a pretty bottle they do make excellent Christmas presents.

INTRODUCTION

This is not so much a recipe as a series of guidelines that I have developed by trial and error. I am happy to set out the variables but you will have to decide just what you wish to achieve. For example, if you are looking for some special oil to invigorate your salad dressings or barbecues you won't be so concerned that it is crystal clear. On the other hand when it comes to Christmas presents, presentation is all.

STRONGLY FLAVOURED OILS

You'll need a 1 litre Le Parfait preserving jar or similar. Put your base 1 litre of sunflower oil into a liquidiser or food processor and add either:

A large bunch of fresh rosemary; or

A large bunch of fresh thyme; or

A head of garlic, roast it first and squeeze each sweet and softened clove from its papery skin; or

A very large bunch of fresh tarragon; or

As much real saffron as you can sensibly afford (3 grams); or

A very large bunch of garden mint.

Then whizz the mixture very briefly; you are seeking to bruise the herbs and chop them up a bit not reduce them to a pulp. Then put the oil and herbs into the jar and seal up tight. Leave it on the window sill (some authorities recommend leaving it in direct sunlight) and give it a shake whenever you remember. After a month most of the herb flavour will be in the oil.

Then you have two choices, you can either strain it off through doubled butter muslin and bottle it, adding a single pretty sprig of the relevant herb for show, or use it just as it is, warts and all.

OILS WITH SOMETHING EXTRA

These combinations are more complex, and rely on a good tasting oil to start with, although the method and provisos are the same as set out earlier:

MIXED HERB OIL

 850 ml (1½ pints) extra virgin olive oil

 150 ml (5 fl oz) walnut oil

 3 sprigs fresh rosemary

 3 sprigs fresh tarragon

 1 tbs black peppercorns

 ½ clove garlic

CHINOIS OIL

 850 ml (1½ pints) groundnut oil

 150 ml (5 fl oz) sesame oil

 Small piece of root ginger, peeled

 Bunch of fresh coriander

 1 tbs Sichuan pepper

SPICED OIL

500 ml (18 fl oz) extra virgin olive oil

500 ml (18 fl oz) sunflower oil

5 green cardamom pods, bruised

1 tsp grated nutmeg

1 cinnamon stick

3 whole green chillies

1 tbs whole black peppercorns

PROVENÇAL OIL

1 litre (1¾ pints) extra virgin olive oil

2 tbs 'herbes de Provence'

½ clove garlic

Lastly, and looking rather out of place here, as it is a recipe that contains not a single drop of oil – chilli sherry. This is the hottest condiment imaginable; it is right up there with West Indian yellow pepper sauce. Should you ever have a casserole or soup that is not behaving itself properly, then the threat of a few drops of this should bring it into line. I keep mine in an old Worcestershire sauce bottle so that I can add it in very, very tiny amounts when the going gets tough. I have included it here because you make it by following much the same principles as used for these herb oils.

INGREDIENTS FOR CHILLI SHERRY
A bottle of fino sherry
125 g (4½ oz) fresh hot chillies

Put the chillies into a liquidiser, add the sherry and pulverise. Keep the mixture in a jar for a month, shaking occasionally. Strain and re-bottle. It may be wise to wear gloves during this operation as getting the chilli sherry near your eyes or other vulnerable parts of your anatomy will cause excruciating pain.

Treat like gelignite, and add very sparingly.

Number Thirty-Five – Kedgersotto

In which we marvel at the iron constitution
needed by the sahibs

As usual, our lust for empire was to blame. The Indians were happily enjoying a dish of rice, onions, lentils and eggs called *Kadgeri* (this name was probably derived from the older Hindi word *Khicari* and is sometimes written *Kitchri*), when along came the sahibs. Unimpressed by this superior sort of dal, they decided that the dish needed that little something. That little English sort of something. Fish! That was it, and in view of the climate, the lack of refrigeration, and the unreliability of the damn natives, smoked haddock would be perfect. And no sooner said than done, there it was – kedgeree, the chosen breakfast dish of the aspirant English middle classes.

My mother used to make a very pleasant kedgeree, from Patna rice, smoked haddock, a white sauce and hard-boiled eggs, on a slice of toast and with a rasher of crisply fried bacon crumbled over the top of it.

Wouldn't it have been splendid if Italy had been a part of the British Empire? Then as well as enjoying better coffee and the joys of pasta and bottom-pinching, we might have invented a kedgeree that ran along risotto lines. Think of it, instead of boiled, drained, long-grain Patna rice, we could start with the fat medium-grained rice of the Po valley. We could cook the rice in something more flavourful than water; we could change the method so that the rice cooked slowly and took on the rich flavours of the haddock. Admittedly it wouldn't finish up with every grain separate, but it would be a fine and luxurious thing. But there's never any point in putting the clock back, better to step out bravely and work up the dish rather than speculate. That's what I did, and that's what this kedgersotto recipe is all about. There are a great many different types of rice available now, basmati (very long grained, nutty, fragrant, almost scented), Patna (long grained), American (long grained), Italian Arborio (medium to short grained), and short-grained pudding rice. For a 'kedgersotto' it is worth searching out Arborio, or another specialist Italian risotto rice. Their medium grains will absorb more liquid than standard long-grain rice and the finished dish will be much creamier in consistency.

Risotto occupies a strange place in the world of science; it is definitely not a solid, and equally definitely not a liquid. Risotto enigmatically bridges these two physical states and therein lies its charm. Kedgersotto has social advantages too. Cooking risotto is a steady and painstaking business which, coupled with the fact that it is at its best the very moment that it is ready, makes it the perfect dish for people whose kitchen and dining-room are one. With a modicum of advance preparation you can stand over the stove looking busy and intense whilst chatting about this and that with your guests until the very moment dinner is served. If you take care, there is very little that can go wrong with 'kedgersotto', and you can claim the credit for your *bon mots* and dinner at the same time.

INTRODUCTION

To make this dish work you are going to need good risotto rice; your first choice should be Italian Arborio (other more esoteric varietal names to look out for are Maratelli, Carnaroli and Roma). Failing that, some of the more pushy supermarkets sell 'risotto rice'. You'll need some fresh eggs, some real cream and some smoked haddock. The only challenge to your ability as a shopper is likely to come in finding decent smoked haddock. There has been a long-running argument over whether smoked haddock should be dyed or not. Yellow or grey: that is the question. To be honest I lean towards undyed but am not dogmatic. Better by far that you make your own mind up and then move on to securing the best possible quality in your chosen fish. I would recommend looking for plump fish not too gnarled or grizzled, and relatively thick so that you end up with nice chunky flakes. Small vacuum-packed fillets would never be more than my last resort.

INGREDIENTS

700 g (1 lb 9oz) smoked haddock

300 g (10½ oz) Arborio rice

1–1.2 litres (1½–2 pints) whole milk

1 small onion finely chopped

75 g (2½ oz) unsalted butter

4 fresh eggs, hard-boiled

142 ml carton double cream

Salt and freshly ground black pepper

METHOD

First, take a large saucepan and put into it the milk and the haddock. Bring it up to a gentle simmer over a period of ten minutes or so, then simmer for about a further minute. Take it off the heat and lift the fish out on to a tray with a slotted spoon. Set the (by now nicely fishy) milk to one side. Using fingers and forks and knives and whatever, take the haddock apart into flakes carefully, discard all the skin, dodgy bits and bones. You should be left with a pile of flaked fish that even the fussiest person should be able to munch through with absolute confidence.

Then take your favourite risotto pan, or indeed any large heavy pan, and melt the butter in it gently. Add the finely chopped onion and sweat until it is translucent and soft. Then add the rice and stir until each grain is well coated with the butter. The rice will probably just start to stick a bit as it begins to cook; don't worry.

Take a ladleful (about a tenth of the total volume) of the milk and stir it into the rice over a low heat. Continue stirring as the liquid is absorbed. Do that again. And again. And once again, until all the milk is in all the rice, or the rice refuses to take up any more. This procedure should take twenty minutes whilst you dazzle your dinner guests with repartee. When you have got a pan full of delicious sludgy rice adjust the seasoning. Be careful with the salt because quite a lot will have come out of the haddock; go for it with the freshly ground black pepper. Then stir in the cream vigorously, the haddock flakes gently, and your chopped hard-boiled eggs hardly at all. Serve and await the plaudits.

You'll quickly find out that 'kedgersotto' is a very nice dish with a very silly name.

Number Thirty-Six – Extraordinarily Scotch Eggs

In which we investigate the
composition of snorkas

In what seems like a past life, I worked for an ad agency that had the rather cruel nickname of the 'Ministry of Advertising'. This ponderous and worthy organisation had imposing premises in the West End of London, and just around the corner was a café where I was sometimes to be found taking breakfast with my art director. This was the setting for my first brush with the nomenclature 'snorka'.

I had grown up under the misapprehension that Mr and Mrs Average called sausages 'Jimmers', as a direct consequence of my father's rather eccentric tendency to recite short, inconsequential, and sometimes rather rude, poems at the slightest prompting. One of these epics went as follows:

> The sausage was a fat one,
> The outside was the skin,
> The inside was a mystery,
> So we called it little Jim.

Ergo, sausages were known as 'Jimmers', and I had never even heard of snorkas. This pleasant little café in St James's, where my art director Paul and I occasionally enjoyed coffee and a bacon sandwich, had a light airy dining-room and would have been perfection were we the only customers. However, due to the proximity of one of the world's premier auction houses, the café also enjoyed the custom of an endless stream of young women, each apparently fresh from the same mould. Sensible skirts, blue jumpers, pearls, and diction so relentless and powerful as to stun a sergeant major. Pausing for a year or so betwixt education and matrimony they put in long hours for short pay, but amongst the right kind of people. They would have been charming if they weren't so very loud: braying on about parties, Henley, Annabel's and so forth. In those days, I occasionally suffered from a twinge of hangover at breakfast time and then the jolly babble of these bright young things would become particularly onerous. Fortunately the man we were to nickname 'Snorkas' was more than a match for the *jeunesse dorée*.

Paul and I were sharing our table with a solidly built gent of about fifty years of age. He had a beard, a copy of *The Times*, an auction catalogue and a navy-blue tweed overcoat. First of all he sat and read his paper, and then ordered 'bacon and eggs and a couple of snorkas'. The tiny Italian lady who took his order was obviously perplexed, so he explained in a force-ten voice, 'Snorkas is the Navy's name for sausages.' At which point Sophie told Emma how she was sick all over Jonty's helicopter on the way to his party in Cumbria. The man called Snorkas was roused by this intrusion, and tapping Sophie on the shoulder commented, 'I don't give a bugger what you did at the weekend.' Then he turned to include Paul and myself, 'And neither do these gentlemen.' We nodded meekly. 'So belt up and drink your coffee.' Then he attacked his plate of snorkas whilst relishing the ensuing silence, and we did likewise.

Even the most reputable snorka is a bit of a gamble. You cannot rely on the contents living up to outward appearances. And as for those plastic rolls simply labelled 'sausage meat', they hardly bear thinking about.

I was forced to reassess sausages when I decided to put a simple starter on the hotel menu. I had a fancy to make tiny Scotch eggs, using quails' eggs wrapped in something savoury. But what? In the end I took the best possible sausage meat available and customised it. And that whim became these 'extraordinarily Scotch eggs'.

INTRODUCTION

These little Scotch eggs make a superb starter with a couple halved and nestling into some crisp green leaves. Or as finger food for buffets. I like to see them served warm, with a nice crisp outside.

You should have no trouble obtaining quails' eggs, but hard-boiling them and peeling them is slightly more testing. First boil them for three minutes, then plunge into cold water before peeling painstakingly in the usual way only on a smaller scale – fiddly work.

You're going to need some sausage meat. Perhaps the most practical way to avoid the anonymous snorka trap is to buy premium pork sausages, either from a trusted butcher or from the supermarket, and take off the skin. This is a very simple task: just hold the whole string of sausages under a running tap and slit each with a knife. You'll find that the water stretches the skins and that they come away cleanly from the meat inside.

In addition you'll require some white breadcrumbs. Home-made are best, though those trendy Japanese ones called *panka* are pretty good. On no account use the dreadful commercial ones that are bright orange and yellow. You will see from the ingredients list that you also need some good, coarse-cut, garlicky pâté. Once again, there is no real substitute for home-made, but if needs must, buy some pâté that fits the above criteria.

If you want to make these Scotch eggs in advance, they'll heat up very acceptably in the oven or microwave – remember not to cut them in half until they're hot.

INGREDIENTS

2 dozen peeled, hard-boiled quails' eggs

700 g (1 lb 9oz) good-quality pork sausages

350 g (12 oz) coarse pâté

2 medium onions, peeled and finely chopped

25 g (1 oz) unsalted butter

2 cloves of garlic

Juice of half a lemon

1 fresh hen's egg

Fresh parsley

Freshly ground black pepper

Groundnut oil for deep frying

METHOD

Fry the onions in the butter until soft, and then put them with the sausage meat, pâté and the lemon juice into a mixing bowl. Crush the garlic and add it; chop about a handful of parsley finely and add that. Then add a couple of turns of black pepper, and the hen's egg which you have beaten up. Use your hands to work everything into a homogeneous mixture. Do not succumb to the temptations of machines, processors or the like – the texture of your little Scotch eggs will be better if the mixture is not pounded to death. Roll each egg in a little plain flour to help the mixture stick and then mould the 'super sausage meat' to the eggs by hand. You are aiming to have a regular coating on each egg just less than 1 cm thick (just over ¼ in). Then roll each Scotch egg in plain white (or *panka*) breadcrumbs to give the end product a crispy coat.

Everything is now ready for deep frying. Use fresh groundnut oil and aim to have it about 335°F or 170°C. Put the eggs into the basket four at a time so that they don't cause a huge temperature drop when you first immerse them. Each batch will take about four minutes, but watch them like a hawk, as they can easily go from crisp nut-brown, to crisp carbon-black! Drain them on kitchen paper and then warm them through, either in the oven or for thirty seconds in a microwave, when you want to serve them. Delicious and diminutive – they're extraordinarily Scotch eggs.

Number Thirty-Seven – From Sloe Gin to Lychee Rum

*In which we prove the adage, 'A secret is
something you tell one person at a time'*

I never liked gin. After an unfortunate and close encounter with a large amount of gin one afternoon whilst still a schoolboy, I have never been able to drink it without attendant feelings of nausea. It's a pity, because every now and then at the height of summer I see someone drinking a long gin and tonic – smoky blue-grey with tinkling ice cubes and jaunty slice of lemon – and I resolve to try one. How could anything that looks so enticing make me feel so ill? But even now, many years after my indiscretion, the smell of gin still makes me uneasy.

The exception to this salutary sensation is sloe gin. I like sloe gin. Not the pallid pink, low-proof stuff you get if you have to buy it over a counter, but the rich red, heart-warming stuff you make yourself. And given certain provisos it is very easy to make. There are three main problems to overcome. First you have to know where there are some sloe bushes; secondly you have to get there before someone else has stripped them bare; and thirdly your cash flow has to cope with a shocking bill for an eyebrow-raising amount of gin.

Sloe bushes are scrubby, thorny, unprepossessing things – the only sure way to identifying them is to catch them in the autumn when they are covered in sloes: beautiful, dusty blue, miniature plumlets. Of course, by then they may well have been picked. So the only sure-fire way to find a good place to pick sloes is if someone blabs. I recommend you express an interest in sloes to all and sundry until someone weakens. In Buxton we were blessed with a diner who not only told us about lychee rum but also unselfishly shared the location of a small forest of productive sloe bushes. I dare not publicise the exact spot, but if you were to find the village of Calton at the southern end of the Peak District, and you then walked through each dale marked on the map nearby you would eventually find the right one (and even if not, you'd enjoy some excellent and invigorating walking).

Some learned authorities say that you should wait until the first frost in late October/early November before picking your suitably weathered sloes. This principle is all very well, but relies on no other enthusiast picking the sloe bushes clean while you wait for frost. Better the sloe in the hand than a no-sloe area.

Another myth that is worth debunking is the tale of the silver needle. In most recipes you tend to be told that each sloe must be pricked all over with a needle. This is not true. You do need to let your gin get from the outside to the inside of each sloe, and that can be accomplished by making a small nick about 5 mm ($\frac{1}{8}$ in) long in each sloe – use a really sharp knife, whichever you would choose to score pork with. But however you go about it, preparing sloes means a long painstaking slog. One year I tried the much vaunted secret short cut of freezing the sloes (with the intention that they would then split and save us the labour). I'm annoyed to report that it didn't work for me.

Sloe gin is so moreish that even though we make a couple of gallons a year, we only bottle it in half bottles, because as night follows day you tend to finish up whatever you open. For those of you with slightly less stamina in the 'pick-from-the-wild' arena I would suggest you try making blackberry brandy, and for those who are quite prepared to buy their raw materials, there are the twin delights of sloe gin's poor cousin, damson gin and the exotic newcomer lychee rum.

INTRODUCTION

Each of the following recipes produces a delicious liqueur. They need to be bottled after about nine months and then aged for as long as you can manage. The most radical improvement comes in the first four or five years, but they go on getting better for ever and ever. (I've enjoyed a splendid forty-year-old sloe gin.) Good luck with the self-control.

Most old recipes for sloe gin suggest the addition of burnt almonds. I have tried this but can report that the end result was no better than you can achieve using natural almond essence. All the recipes are based on proportions except for the weight of sugar to add which relates to volume of spirit.

SLOE GIN INGREDIENTS

Sloes

An equal volume of reputable gin

Caster sugar at a rate of 250 g (9 oz) per bottle of gin

Almond essence at a rate of ½ tsp per bottle of gin

SLOE GIN METHOD

Nick each sloe with a small sharp knife, and put them in a jar. We use a one-gallon demijohn but any sealable jar will do; the size will depend on how ambitious your production is. Then add the sugar, gin and almond essence in the proportions set out. Put the jar in a dark place and give it an occasional shake. After nine months or so, strain through doubled butter muslin and bottle. Cork traditionally and keep for as long as you are able before sampling.

DAMSON GIN INGREDIENTS

Damsons

An equal volume of reputable gin

Caster sugar at a rate of 300 g (10½ oz) per bottle of gin

Almond essence at a rate of ½ tsp per bottle of gin

DAMSON GIN METHOD

Proceed exactly as for sloe gin.

BLACKBERRY BRANDY INGREDIENTS
Ripe blackberries

An equal volume of reputable brandy

Caster sugar at a rate of 200 g (7 oz) per bottle of brandy

A whole vanilla pod

BLACKBERRY BRANDY METHOD
Mash the blackberries thoroughly with a potato masher, add the brandy and mix well. Then transfer to a jar with the other ingredients and treat as sloe gin. When you come to bottle do not worry about the cloudiness of the drink. Blackberries are very bitty and dusty; when you finally serve one of your treasured bottles, just decant it like vintage port leaving the sediment behind and you'll find you have a wonderful, deep red, perfectly clear liqueur.

LYCHEE RUM INGREDIENTS
Peeled, ripe, fresh lychees

An equal volume of golden (not dark) rum

Caster sugar at a rate of 225 g (8 oz) per bottle of rum

LYCHEE RUM METHOD
Follow the guiding principles of the sloe gin method. The lychees should be peeled, but the stones should be left in. The rum should be one of the

mellow yellow West Indian rums like Mount Gay or Cockspur. Keep the lychees and rum in the jar for a year and then bottle. If you have any problems with sediment simply decant. The end product is amazingly highly scented although the flavour is not intense – it is excellent for adding an exotic perfume to a straightforward fruit salad.

Number Thirty-Eight – Fillet of Lamb with Lentils

In which we commune with nature and the
dear little lambs – roasted pink

Imagine you could step backwards through time as easily as through your kitchen door. Go on, take an awayday to the 1930s. No frozen peas in January, you'd have to wait the winter out for the first young peas of summer. Broad beans couldn't be hurried either, nor new potatoes or tomatoes. And there would be no supermarket Brussels sprouts in June. Without the freezer (and the airfreight companies), seasonal foods would still be seasonal and eagerly awaited. The first vegetables and fruits of each season would have a cachet all of their own. We've given all that up for the sake of convenience. You can now not only buy anything at any time of the year, but you can also buy it in miniature, and in a new range of designer colours and types.

This fate has also befallen meat. What about spring lamb? When sheep lived outdoors and tupping was a more erogenous and less artfully timed affair, the lambs were born to coincide with the show of new grass in the spring. They suckled their way through April and May while their mothers enjoyed the best grass of the year. As a consequence, spring lamb was the connoisseur's choice. Young, sweet and nutty.

Today you hear of some farmers starting lambing at the beginning of December. The little chaps are born indoors, fed indoors and live indoors. They are also on the market early enough to steal a march (no pun intended) on their more tardy cousins. Is it any wonder that across the UK the lambs in butchers' shops tend to be getting smaller, leaner, and blander tasting? I can offer no solution to this problem, save invoking the power of market forces. If everyone insisted on proper lamb then proper lamb is what they'd get. So confront your butcher, ask him for a lamb that has seen a bit of life and you'll taste the difference.

Fillet of lamb with lentils is a simple dish that relies on combining two distinct textures – the tender noisette of lamb sits on top of a sauce-cum-purée of lentils. The lentil mixture should taste nutty, and the lamb fresh and juicy. Having first got your butcher to own up to a fat, young, free-range lamb, you then face the problem of explaining to him just which bit of it you want. It is usually simpler to do the butchery yourself, and thankfully it is a relatively easy job, but failing that you can explain it to him carefully. You should remember at all times that if pushed to sell you a fillet of lamb, he will probably resort to offering a piece of boned shoulder or best end of neck, and delicious though they may be, they are not what I am referring to.

What you want is the sausage-shaped eye of absolutely lean meat that runs lengthwise through a loin of lamb. To procure it at home simply buy all the loin chops in a piece and cut it out carefully. Everything that remains can go for stews and stocks. If you get the butcher to carry out this procedure he will charge you for the whole loin anyway, and then some. Asking for this particular piece of meat is inviting a serious bill, however tactfully you handle it, so if you are in the throes of an economy drive turn the page briskly and cook something else. There is something about the concept of just eating the very best bit that sets even the most helpful butcher's charging dial to 'stun'. As for portion control I can only offer the valuable rule of thumb that you should allow 12 cm (5 in) of loin fillet per person.

This dish should present the diner with some plainly cooked medallions of tender lamb sitting atop a pool-or-mound of lentil kind-of-sauce. You will end up tempting your guest with a choice of three equally delightful mouthfuls – lamb; lentils; and the two together. Even taking into account the potential arguments with your butcher, this dish is well worth trying.

INTRODUCTION

Having dwelt at some length on the provenance of the lamb, it only remains to comment on the lentils. Generally speaking, lentils have a rather bad name in the UK. This is in consequence of the role they played in archetypal vegetarian food (mainly in television sitcoms).

Fortunately that no longer seems to be the case, and any supermarket worth its salt now sells brown and green lentils. These are sometimes billed as 'Tuscan' lentils, and sometimes as lentils from Puy in France. As this is essentially a two-stage recipe, with the meat being presented on, but not cooked with, the lentils, I will deal with each element in turn.

THE LAMB

Having obtained 12 cm (5 in) of lamb per diner as we discussed earlier, you should then cut it into medallions if your chosen cooking method is frying. Your 12 cm section will make four nice medallions; they need to be this thick so that you can cook them nicely brown on the outside, fading to a gentle pink in the very middle. Do not start to cook them until you have got the lentils to your liking. When you are ready, fry the medallions in a tiny amount of unsalted butter. Exactly how long you give them will depend so much upon the foibles of your particular pan and cooker that I wouldn't hazard a guess. You need to cook them to the point immediately before they are done to your liking, then take them away from the heat, cover them with a bit of foil and rest them for five minutes. If you elect to grill the meat then you should cook it in the piece. The same comments as to done-ness apply, and you should then cut the fillet up into medallions after it has been rested.

INGREDIENTS FOR THE LENTILS

200 g (7 oz) lentils

2 medium onions, finely chopped

25 g (1 oz) unsalted butter

300 ml (10 fl oz) whole milk

50 ml (2 fl oz) double cream

Salt and freshly ground black pepper

½ tsp cumin seeds

METHOD

Put the lentils into a pan with a good covering of water and no salt, then boil until nearly tender. Drain and reserve. Next, fry the onions in the butter until they are starting to colour. Put three quarters of the lentils, the onions and the milk into a food processor and whizz until smooth. Add the cream, add the cumin seeds and then season to taste. Return the purée to the pan and add the whole lentils you have saved. Heat through very gently and stir from time to time.

Serve the lamb on top of the lentils.

Number Thirty-Nine – Curiously Hot Horseradish

*In which we discuss the best way to pass the
night before one's wedding day*

The night before my wedding day found me head down in a ditch soundly cursing my mother's best border fork on which I had just broken a tine. One of the useful tips which should be included in scouting manuals and the like is that you can often find horseradish growing at the roadside. This intelligence is the product of a bygone age when every cottage had a front garden leading to the road and every front garden had a clump of horseradish growing in it. Even though the cottage and its garden have long since been reabsorbed into the surrounding countryside, the horseradish remains – as any gardener will tell you, once horseradish is established, you've got it for good. This tip for sourcing horseradish is doubly valuable as by nature it is a notoriously slow-growing plant, and takes many years to grow its roots to a size that makes for simple peeling. The roots you may scrump at the roadside are likely to have been left undisturbed for some time, because not everyone is deranged enough to go grubbing about there.

Anyway, our wedding breakfast was to include a splendid set of fore-ribs of beef cooked rare, and, interfering as always, I had purloined the border fork as my first step towards making horseradish sauce. Genuine horseradish sauce: the stuff that makes the eyes water and the nose run.

Genuine horseradish sauce is far removed from some of those strange jars of tasteless glop you find in supermarkets (at all costs avoid those listing turnip among the ingredients). Real horseradish is quite danger-ous stuff. Pliny recommends its use as a medicine and later generations of herbalists have pressed it into service for application to blackheads and pimples – personally, I should need to be very worried about my complexion before I was moved to slap horseradish sauce over it.

Proper horseradish sauce is a fierce and volatile concoction. Only when the vapour first catches the back of your throat and your eyes start to run in protest will you know that you have got it absolutely right – it is a curiously hot sauce!

INTRODUCTION

First catch your horseradish. Then take a good deal of care over peeling and grating it. One of those French vegetable peelers (called speed peelers) is the ideal tool to strip off the outside, but then there is no substitute for barking your knuckles on an old-fashioned grater – the fine side, unless you have one of those new-style, and very sharp, microplane devices. After handling horseradish, be particularly careful to wash your hands scrupulously, otherwise you run the risk of wiping your eyes without thinking and suffering the consequent discomfort. Fortunately you don't need much horseradish to make a decent bowl of sauce. Unfortunately it will only keep for a few days.

To make a good sauce you also need some authentic English mustard. When you make up yellow English mustard, it gets hotter and hotter for the first twenty minutes you let it stand, as the various chemical reactions take place, so it is wise to make your mustard half an hour before you need it. I like to make mustard with beer not water, and to add a drop of olive oil and a pinch of salt. Whether by luck or by judgement this mixture doesn't seem to skin over so quickly.

INGREDIENTS

40 g (1½ oz) finely grated fresh horseradish root

1 tbs made-up English mustard

1 tbs white sugar

2 tbs white-wine vinegar

1 tsp salt

284 ml carton double cream

METHOD

If you try this recipe and you find that the resulting sauce is either chokingly hot or demeaningly mild simply adjust the amounts of horseradish and mustard accordingly. Start by putting the horseradish, mustard, sugar and vinegar into a bowl and mixing together thoroughly. Let the mixture stand for ten minutes. Then stir in the double cream and it will quickly thicken up. Check seasoning and adjust. Pop it into the fridge and wait for the beef with extra anticipation.

Number Forty – Cassoulet

*In which we concern ourselves with a dish so
formidable it can only be eaten at lunchtime*

I would not be surprised if someone somewhere has written an entire
book about cassoulet. Everyone has their own opinion. You'll find
recipes that suggest cassoulet is not authentic if it omits pork; salt pork;
confit; partridge; Toulouse sausages; garlic sausage; shoulder of lamb;
neck of lamb; breast of lamb; goose; duck; mutton; beans from Arpajon;
beans from Soissons; breadcrumbs; tomatoes.

Many believe that cassoulet cannot be the real thing unless it was
made in Carcassone, or Toulouse, or Castelnaudray. At this point you
may be sure of only one thing, either everybody is right or nobody is! I
subscribe to the former point of view. My mother used to serve a huge
pot of what she called Boston Baked Beans every year at our Guy
Fawkes Night party, and even that adhered to most of the tenets of
cassoulet. It is our misfortune that beans have played such a relatively
small part in our national cuisine. Mr Heinz swept through our kitchens
and more adventurous bean dishes were reduced to their lowest common denominator by that great leveller, the mass market.

Cassoulet is the supreme dish to set before a tried and tested trencherman. It calls for maximum effort on the part of the digestive system, so much so that in its homeland it is almost always consumed only at lunchtime. This is a pretty sensible guideline, as anyone who has tried to sleep after a sublimely rich and ponderously heavy cassoulet can confirm.

When we put it on our restaurant menu we took liberties with the purists' recipes. My interpretation has no crust of breadcrumbs; no Toulouse sausages; no lamb; no confit – but for all that it is a plateful to be taken seriously.

However, we did make use of a secret weapon, *haricots géants*; I purchased them on a trip to France from the co-op grocery in a little village outside Evreux, and until my supply ran out they gave our cassoulet a significant edge. When you next eat cassoulet in France just marvel at the size of the beans: each bean is usually about 2 cm (¾ in) long. The haricots on supermarket shelves in the UK are midgets by comparison. Anyhow, there they were near Evreux – *haricots géants* – they were not butter beans, they were just huge haricots. I bought the shop's entire stock, and they cooked up to melting deliciousness like the refried beans you can sometimes get in good Mexican restaurants. With the clarity of vision that attends hindsight, I suspect that these beans were the ones known by Greeks as *gigandes* and increasingly available in the UK.

Aside from the beans and the meats, the other crucial factor in the creation of cassoulet is the fat, and whilst confit seems to me to be altogether too expensive a delicacy to use as a mere adjunct to a pot of beans, goose fat is an amazing asset – hardly surprisingly when you think of its primary role, which is making the best roast potatoes in Christendom. So when you next have a roast goose, think cassoulet, or failing that, do as I do and include a duck early on in your cassoulet plans.

INTRODUCTION

You can't be too careful with beans. The beans for your cassoulet should be the largest, whitest beans you can get hold of. At best that means *gigandes*; at worst that means ordinary haricots; and somewhere in the middle lie cannellini beans. In the category *acceptable also-rans* are pinto beans and borlotti beans which are the right shape if not the right colour. Tinned beans will not do. The beans face a long haul in a cassoulet and if they are already cooked they'll flag well before the end. So buy your beans dry and watch out, even dried beans deteriorate with time. New season's beans come into the shops by the autumn (given a shop with a halfway decent turnover) and by the following August they will be getting pretty hard. However, if you're the kind of person who can contemplate cassoulet in August, something as esoteric as bean-hardness is unlikely to put you off.

When my recipe mentions fat pork, what it means is either a fat piece of belly pork or a sheet of *bark* – the back fat complete with skin that butcher's sometimes wrap around the breasts of pheasants. When the recipe mentions pork, what you need is a nice piece of shoulder or leg. The final wild card in the recipe is *zwiecka*, which is a firm, Polish, garlic sausage about 4 cm (1½ in) in diameter which you can get from delicatessens.

INGREDIENTS

500 g (1 lb 2 oz) dried gigandes beans

A large fat duck

500 g (1 lb 2 oz) back fat pork

500 g (1 lb 2 oz) shoulder pork

500 g (1 lb 2 oz) *zwiecka* sausage

6 cloves of garlic

3 medium onions, finely chopped

2 whole onions

2 carrots

2 leeks

1 tbs honey

Salt and freshly ground black pepper

METHOD – DAY ONE

Having got hold of the best possible beans, pick them over, and put them to soak in cold water. Prick the duck all over to let the fat through the skin, and then roast it breast side down on a grid in a medium oven until cooked. Reserve the duck fat. Carve the duck into pieces, and use the remaining carcass and odds and ends to make a simple stock with the two whole onions (quartered in their skins), the leeks and carrots.

METHOD – DAY TWO

Rinse the beans and put them in a pan, cover with water, bring to the boil and after ten minutes strain the water off and replace it with the stock. Bring the beans to the boil once again and then turn down and simmer until the beans are nearly cooked – in about an hour's time. It is worth noting that when you are cooking beans you should never add salt, or anything wildly acidic (like tomatoes) as they will make the bean skins go leathery; you should also heat up any liquids you are going to add during the cooking process as adding something cold also makes for tough beans.

Take six tablespoonfuls of the duck fat and melt it in a frying pan. Add the finely chopped onions and the crushed garlic, cook gently. When they're cooked, put your duck fat, onions and garlic into the bottom of the large heavy casserole you are going to use for your cassoulet. Add the beans layered with the back fat pork, together with 300 ml (10 fl oz) of the stock that you cooked the beans in.

Put the lid on and put it in a low oven, gas mark 2 / 300°F / 150°C, for three hours.

METHOD – DAY THREE

Cut your shoulder pork into sensible chunks and fry them quickly in a little duck fat. Open your casserole and remove the lumps of fat pork, scraping the beans and gunge off carefully into the pot. If it is *bark* put it out for the birds, if it is belly then challenge your ingenuity to find a good secondary use for it. Put the chunks of pork into the beans and cook in a low oven, gas mark 2 / 300°F / 150°C. Look at the pot every hour, and if the beans look impossibly dry then add a little boiling water. After two hours add the pieces of duck and the *zwiecka* cut into 4 cm (1 ½ in) lengths. After a further hour stir in the tablespoonful of honey and your remaining duck fat. Do not mind if the beans are starting to break up and form a lovely glutinous mass. After half an hour season carefully with salt and pepper, and then leave the lid off the pot for the last half-hour so that your cassoulet develops a nice crisp crust. If anything in this procedure strikes you as wrong, I urge you to change it to suit yourself; cassoulet is what you make it and all are equally genuine.

And remember, lunchtimes only!

Number Forty-One – Sesame and Tomato Bread

In which we overhaul the adage,
'Let them eat cake'

There is a body of learned opinion convinced that when Marie Antoinette said, 'If they have no bread, why then let them eat cake,' she was in fact referring to brioche. Then the debate descends into an argument about whether brioche is in fact a sweet bread or a plain cake, which corollary seems to defeat the object of the exercise. These discussions could never have happened in Britain. For a long while, nearly all bread was unspeakably nasty, and confusing it with cake in any form was quite impossible. Like keg beers, for decades bread had been standardised, enhanced and robbed of every natural virtue in pursuit of a longer shelf life. The big bakers used steam ovens, improvers and bleaches to make loaves that were identical and, to many people's taste, identically nasty. I remember walking through the backwoods of Camden Town one day and passing a glowering Victorian edifice that was HQ for the huge bakery which rejoiced in the name ABC. I had always thought this choice of name was a foresighted attempt by some Victorian plutocrat to get his company a premier listing in telephone directories, but there on the wall was a brass plate bearing the legend Aerated Bread Company. Which only goes to show that one generation's advertising slogan can be another's embarrassment.

Times have certainly changed: nowadays Pain Poîlane is sold in London; ciabatta can be found on supermarket shelves; and craft bakers command a premium for their products. It was in this spirit of adventure that I worked up this recipe for sesame and tomato bread, and very tasty it is too. It certainly could never be mistaken for cake as it has a nutty, savoury taste, and the tang from the tomatoes echoes the tang you get from a really good sourdough bread.

The key to this bread lies in using sun-dried tomatoes. These amazing little flavour bombs are now rather old hat, so try and get high quality ones (given there are oven-baked imitations on the marketplace). They should be tomatoes that have been picked, dried on a rack in the sun, and then packed in oil to preserve them, although by going to an authentic Italian store you can sometimes buy them loose, just dried. The concentration of flavour is magnificent, and sun-dried tomatoes in this guise are a splendid addition to all kinds of casseroles, soups and salads – so much nicer than that violently coloured, and wildly acidic, tomato purée you get in tubes and tins.

This sesame and tomato bread has a strong character of its own and makes a good starter if you team it with some fresh mozzarella and some good oil; or bresaola; or even crudités. It is also a fine excuse to splash out on a baking stone, if you haven't already got one. I was given one by my wife for a birthday present some years ago and I wouldn't be without it. These baking stones, or pizza stones as they are sometimes known, are simply pieces of thick, non-stick, ovenproof ceramic upon which you bake your bread or pizza. It enables you to recreate the wonderful crust you get on the bottom of bread when you are able to bake directly on the hot oven floor.

INTRODUCTION

For this recipe you need decent sun-dried tomatoes; do remember to drain them well. You also need sesame oil and sesame seeds – most supermarkets stock the former, and most health-food shops the latter. As to the flour, any strong white bread flour will do. For further general discussion of breadmaking, cast your eye back to Recipe 1. If you are using leftover dough from that recipe, just add a quarter the quantity of sesame oil given here with the tomatoes, and work together before putting the dough to rise.

INGREDIENTS

700 g (1 lb 9oz) strong white flour
25 g (1 oz) fresh yeast
425 ml (15 fl oz) hand hot, warm water
12 g (½ oz) white sugar

2 tbs sesame oil

200 g pack of sun-dried tomatoes in oil

50 g (2 oz) white sesame seeds

A level tsp of salt

METHOD

Add the yeast, sugar and sesame oil to the water, stir well, and put to one side while you sift the salt and flour together into your mixing bowl. Then gradually add the liquid to the flour until you have a dough. Get your hands in it and you'll find that pretty quickly it will all come together and pull away from the bowl. Transfer operations to a work surface and knead the dough. Relax and enjoy it, you are simply pulling and pushing the gluten into shape. After about ten minutes or so you'll find the texture of the dough changes, becoming more elastic. When you think the dough is ready, cut the carefully drained dried tomatoes into shreds and add them. Carry on kneading until they are evenly distributed throughout the dough. Wash, and lightly oil, your big mixing bowl and return the dough to it. Cover the bowl with some clingfilm, and put it in a warmish part of the kitchen to rise – it should double in size. This procedure may take two to three hours.

To bake the loaf you need either a stone or a large baking sheet. Whichever you choose it will need the same preparation – oiling with a little sesame oil. Then take your dough and 'knock it back'. This makes for a uniform distribution of the bubbles within the bread and a good texture in the final loaf. Then make the loaf into a flat oval and lay it on the prepared stone. Cover the whole as best you can with an upturned bowl, and leave it in a warm part of the room for another hour or so. It should 'prove', that is to say that the yeast will resume its work and the loaf will increase in size once again. Before baking, brush the top of the loaf with a little milk, then cut a cross in the top and sprinkle on the white sesame seeds. Put the stone into a pre-heated oven, gas mark 7 / 425°F / 220°C. The bread should be done after forty-five minutes, so have a look at it after half an hour. If it's getting very dark on top don't be afraid to turn it over. You can tell when the loaf is cooked by turning it over and tapping the bottom; if it's done you'll be rewarded with a nice hollow knocking sound. Take the loaf out, and put it on a rack to cool for at least twenty minutes. It'll be difficult keeping your hands off it, as bread is so delicious hot, and merely smelling it will usually galvanise even the most jaded palate.

Number Forty-Two – Pâté

*In which we marvel
at the changing tastes of Britain*

One of the pleasures of working in advertising is having access to the reels of bygone commercials that tell the story of a brand's development. Television compilation programmes have been screaming out for such material and it now enjoys a much wider audience than before; but it's pleasant to find yourself laughing at a gentle anachronism rather than a savage attack. When I worked on the Mattessons account we came across a particularly jolly series of ancient commercials structured around the deathless catchphrase 'I say . . . Pat ay.'

Before it became a minor subdivision of a mighty multinational, Mattessons was the brainchild of Mr Mattes and his son, and their success stemmed from an unerring ability to make what was then seen as horrid continental food, full of garlic and other unmentionables, palatable to the English. He was so successful that pretty soon the research surveys showed that Mattessons was seen as British through and through. So those bygone commercials depicting bowler-hatted gents eating pâté (by today's standards the product would be considered to be meat paste) seem to have worked.

What Mr Mattes was wrestling with was the strangely inconsistent attitude of the British towards garlic. For hundreds of years – until the Romans introduced the onion to these shores – Britons had only leeks and garlic to add any kind of savoury punch to a dish. Then garlic slid from popularity, being lumped together with all things foreign in the prevailing mood of post-war suspicion. Finally the wheel turned full circle and for a time garlic mushrooms topped the tables as the UK's preferred starter, displacing the incumbent of many years standing – the prawn cocktail.

To most people pâté is the term for what the French refer to as terrine, or very formally, pâté à terrine. If we are irritatingly pedantic, then a pâté should have a pastry base and lid, and is broadly speaking what we would call a pie. To confuse matters still further, there are quite a few British delicacies that a well-meaning French chef could legitimately say look a lot like the inside of a pâté à terrine – meat loaf, some brawns, various potted meats, and that Scottish delicacy hough.

Perhaps this is why my pâté recipe – well, terrine actually – borrows from my mother's picnic loaf; from my love of garlic; and from Jane Grigson's book *Charcuterie and French Pork Cookery*. At the hotel, we served this starter with a miniature pot of home-made chutney and it was very well received.

There are two really tricky steps towards making the perfect terrine –

or pâté. First the various ingredients must be cut up in such a way that they give a good coarse texture to the finished product, and secondly the oven heat and timing must be carefully regulated to avoid over-cooking. It is an irksome truth that only with practice will you achieve consistency. Whilst it seemed like a great chore to make a new terrine every week for the restaurant, it gave me the opportunity to fine-tune this recipe. So the perfect pâté is something you can aspire to as a long-term objective. You should make it, keep it a week for the flavours to settle, and then eat it during the week you start the next one. An ongoing programme.

A couple of specialist bits of kit will help you in your pâté-making mission. An electronic probe thermometer (this will be a godsend for lots of other cooking too, from getting rare beef exactly as you like it, to checking the exact setting point of jam). And a pair of classical, white troughs for making pâté in. I favour the 'narrow gauge' ones, rectangular and about 30 cm (12 in) long, 10 cm (4 in) deep, and 8 cm (3 in) wide.

INTRODUCTION
The quality of your pâté will directly reflect how well you get on with your butcher. There is nothing wildly odd on the ingredients list but the better the quality of what you start with, then the better the pâté at the end. You should be buying each of the meats 'in the piece', rather than

sliced (i.e. they need to be at least 3 cm [1 in] thick – though we'll talk about cutting them up later). Here are some notes on each of them.

The lean pork should be cut from the shoulder, or from a leg steak, you don't want white, wet, supermarket meat, you want some tasty well-grown porker. The hard pork fat is what is also known as back fat; or flare; or speck in delicatessens. It should be hard! The lean smoky bacon should be a piece of dry, lean, smoked bacon. Home-cured short back if at all possible. If not, a single 5 cm (2 in) slice across a side of ordinary smoked back bacon will do. If you can get veal, then 'pie veal' is fine, but always choose English 'bobby', or rose, veal rather than the flabby Dutch stuff. If you prefer rabbit, then wild rabbit is better than farmed. If you can get, and can afford, calf's liver . . . all well and good, if not you can substitute lamb's liver. Don't use pig's liver as it tastes altogether too piggy. Frozen chicken livers are an acceptable second best to fresh ones.

INGREDIENTS

450 g (1 lb) lean pork
200 g (7 oz) hard pork fat
200 g (7 oz) lean smoky bacon
200 g (7 oz) veal or rabbit
200 g (7 oz) calf's liver
100 g (3½ oz) chicken livers

50 ml (2 fl oz) brandy

50 ml (2 fl oz) red wine

1 large fresh egg

50 ml (2 fl oz) double cream

1 clove of garlic

Pounded mace

Salt and freshly ground black pepper

METHOD– DAY ONE

Take your main meats – pork, veal or rabbit, bacon, and hard back fat. How you deal with these will determine the final texture of your terrine. The pork, and veal or rabbit, need to be cut into little batons – about 2 cm (¾ in) long and 5 mm (¼ in) square. This is fiddly but worthwhile; if you mince this meat or machine-chop it, then your pâté will end up as sludge. Take your smoky bacon and remove the lean eye of meat. This needs to be cut into 5 mm (¼ in) cubes, as does the hard back fat, after you've taken off any skin. You now have two lots of batons, and two lots of cubes. Put them all into a bowl with the brandy, red wine, a few twists of freshly ground black pepper and a couple of teaspoonfuls of pounded mace. Mix everything thoroughly with your hands, then cover the bowl with clingfilm and consign it to the fridge for twenty-four hours.

METHOD– DAY TWO

You now have to make the 'farce' part of your pâté, and here I do like using a food processor. Whizz together the calf's liver, the chicken liver, the egg, the cream, and add the garlic after crushing it. Season this mixture by adding 2 teaspoonfuls of salt and then check by poaching a teaspoon full of the 'farce' in boiling water and tasting it; or cooking off a teaspoonful in the microwave. You will have to use your skill and judgement at this point because only you know the saltiness of the bacon you have waiting in the marinade.

Mix the 'farce', and the 'meats' together carefully; this is best done with the fingers, a sublimely messy job. You are now ready to assemble everything in your long terrine dish. Fill the dish to within 2.5 cm (1 in) of the rim and cut a strip of silicone parchment that fits perfectly on the surface of the pâté (like those circles of paper you put on to the very surface of jam when potting it). Then seal the terrine by wrapping it in a double sheet of foil.

Stand your terrine in a large pan of water that comes nearly up to the top, and cook it in a slow oven – gas mark 3 / 325°F / 160°C. Check it after two hours; it should not take more than three hours maximum. You can tell when it is done by the old-fashioned technique: peel back the foil and see whether the juices are running clear and the pâté is shrinking away from the sides of the dish. Or you can take a probe thermometer and shove it through the foil and parchment into the heart of the pâté. When the very middle has reached 120°F or 60°C, all will be well.

Then take the terrine out of the bain-marie and when it is cold replace the foil on top and put it into the fridge for a week to mature. It should not need weighting down. Remember exactly what you have done (if it is not too outrageous a suggestion, perhaps you could keep notes) and then next time try your own improvements: more garlic; less garlic; veal and rabbit; cook it longer. Pretty soon it will be your own pâté recipe, and you can claim all the credit you so richly deserve.

Number Forty-Three – Sensible Salad

In which we ponder the virtuous path

Diet. Unless they are shareholders in the Dr Atkins corporation the very word strikes a chord in overworked consciences throughout the land. It is so easy to find yourself in a position where you are always on a diet. Where does one diet end and the next begin? Are break outs part of the diet or part of the lapses? This is not as solipsistic as it sounds; there are awesome statistical implications if you are trying to keep a faithful record of calories consumed.

My mother was brought up near Axminster in east Devon, and despite her tendency never to ruin a good tale by sticking solely to the truth, I tend to believe her story about dieting. It appears that some time before the Second World War, when 'going on a diet' was a relatively new and radical alternative treatment, the local doctor called to see how a particularly solid farmer's wife was coping with the new diet he had recommended. He was rather surprised to see the lady in question making short work of a couple of large pork chops and a small Everest of buttery mashed potato. Mastering his irritation, he asked in somewhat caustic tones, 'How's the diet, Mrs Endicott?' To which enquiry he received the comforting reply, 'Oh, I've had my diet, thank you. This is my dinner.'

I have had my share of diets, and probably more than my share of dinners. When we are really trying hard, we adopt this sensible salad as the main plank of our attack. I make it by the washing-up bowlful. It is absolutely delicious and, if you can sidestep the crispy skin of a freshly roast chicken and confine yourself to a less than gargantuan portion of the meat and a surfeit of this salad, you'll be able to make significant advances in the ongoing diet war.

Like so many salads, this is really just a very clever dressing that works well with greens and any other bits and pieces you care to add.

As with other of my more *ad hoc* recipes, I have set out a list of candidates for inclusion in this salad. It's by no means definitive, and is not attuned to the contents of your particular store cupboard. I have also appended some estimates as to the calorific content of the dish. This is only a guide, as quite a lot will depend on the exact brands you purchase, and the exact quantities and combinations you decide upon. I just hope that this recipe will raise a glimmer of hope in a world otherwise bounded by an endless procession of eggs or low-fat, even lower-taste, cottage cheese.

INTRODUCTION

To compose the salad you need a nice balance of colours, and a range of textures. It is an unfortunate fact that a mixed salad like this can accommodate a surprisingly vast quantity of dressing without becoming sloppy, as there are so many little bits each of whose surfaces can be covered. So don't cheat and make up extra dressing. The recipe makes use of a good-quality low-calorie mayonnaise, and low-calorie fruit yoghurt – so pick the brand you favour and check the kcal content. The quantities given here are sufficient for a small washing-up bowlful of sensible salad, you only need the washing-up bowl to give you enough room to mix the ingredients thoroughly. Thankfully you are not obliged to serve from it.

INGREDIENTS FOR THE DRESSING

100 g (3½ oz) good-quality, light, low-cal mayonnaise

300 kcal

125 g pot low-calorie fruit yoghurt (pick a tangy one)

40 kcal

½ clove garlic (crushed very finely)   2 kcal

2 good dashes Worcestershire sauce   2 kcal

1 tbs white-wine vinegar   2 kcal

½ tsp salt

Total 346 kcal

METHOD

Shake everything together in a jar with a lid. The chemicals and lecithin which the manufacturers have put in the yoghurt and the mayonnaise will quickly emulsify everything. The result will be an amazingly thick and creamy dressing.

OTHER INGREDIENTS

Pick what you fancy, by all means – three from the first section and then two from the second and one from the third is a fair guideline.

A whole iceberg lettuce, shredded	40 kcal
200 g (7 oz) fresh celery	16 kcal
A whole raw green, red or yellow pepper, chopped finely	20 kcal
300 g (10½ oz) tomatoes, chopped finely	42 kcal
300 g (10½ oz) raw mushrooms, chopped finely	42 kcal
300 g (10 oz) broccoli florets, boiled and let go cold	54 kcal
200 g (7 oz) French beans, boiled, cooled and chopped	21 kcal
200 g (7 oz) bean sprouts	18 kcal
100 g (3½ oz) cooked sweetcorn, drained	76 kcal

100 g (3½ oz) cooked kidney beans, drained	121 kcal
100 g (3½ oz) cooked flageolet beans, drained	110 kcal
200 g (7 oz) chopped beetroot	70 kcal
1 avocado, peeled, stoned and chopped	120 kcal
2 crisp eating apples, cored and chopped	100 kcal
100 g (3½ oz) dried apricots, chopped	180 kcal
50 g (2 oz) sultanas	120 kcal

So as the more able mathematicians among you will have computed by now your washing-up bowlful of salad will have cost you between 650 and 900 kcal depending on how wild your particular choices were. I don't know how much salad you can eat, but supposing two people managed to eat it all, they could still have got away with as little as 325 kcal per head and that leaves ample allowance spare for a lean grilled pork, or some chicken.

Though it's unlikely that there will ever be enough leeway to enjoy the crisp golden skin of a freshly roast chicken – more's the pity.

Number Forty-Four – Cold Springs Chutney

In which we meditate on economic matters

When we opened the doors of our restaurant we did so on a rising tide of good intentions. Real damask tablecloths and napkins; large tables; comfortable chairs; casseroles served in the pot; terrine from the dish so that diners could have a little more if they wished – in short, everything you'd expect from a small family restaurant in France. As we learnt the depressing truth about the dining public we had to retrench, and one of the first casualties was placing the pâté terrine on the table. People were either shy and unable to cope with the responsibility of serving themselves, or happy to serve themselves and unable to cope with their greed. If they had always eaten everything they took I wouldn't have minded, it was having to throw away large hunks of pâté that had been cut from the terrine and then nibbled at before being left on the plate.

We also served home-made chutney with pâté, assigning to it the role that in France is reserved for cornichons. It was incredibly popular, and finally we used to plate up two slices of terrine and add a miniature pot of chutney and send it out. Even then some people complained of being over-faced by pâté and running out of chutney.

Chutney is yet another instance of the valuable legacy of the Raj. By 1845 Eliza Acton set out recipes for chatney, and in doing so was a good deal more faithful to the original Hindustani term chatni, meaning strong spices, than we are today. In the nineteenth century, chutney was essentially a thick sauce rather than the combination of pieces and liquid that it is today, and was used for adding to things rather than as an accompaniment. This recipe for Cold Springs chutney is a domesticated version of the one that used to be so greatly admired in the restaurant.

Unfortunately, when you have domestic levels of production everything immediately becomes more work-intensive. No longer can you use the excellent three-litre tins of green apple or apricot purée; the 600 gram tubs of puréed root ginger; the bags containing 1 kg of peeled garlic cloves! All that prep now has to be done by hand.

Most years we make a batch of 'dangerous Christmas chutney', jars of which do sterling service as Christmas presents. And every year happy recipients ask why we don't turn professional and market chutneys for a living? As they point out, home-made chutney is so much nicer than the bought stuff. Whilst their logic is impeccable, their grasp of retail economics is not. The catch-22 with chutney is the same as the one with Christmas puddings; the end product is only as good to eat as the ingredients you make it with. If you run a business you expect to sell your chutney for three times the cost of those ingredients (one to pay for the ingredients; two to pay for your overheads: staff, pots, labels, gas, distribution, etc.; and three to become your profit). You then trot your jars to the shop where the shopkeeper needs to make 40 percent on what he pays you. This means that a jar of chutney whose ingredients only cost you £1.50 would be retailing for £6.30, which is on the pricey side. No wonder everyone puts up with mass-produced chutneys, and no wonder mass-producers use only the cheaper ingredients. So it should come as no surprise to anyone that home-made chutney is much nicer than bought. Try this Cold Springs chutney and see for yourself.

INTRODUCTION

There's a good deal of preparation work involved in chutney-making, and it is important that once you have started you press on, as that's the way to lock in maximum flavour. So set aside a day when you're prepared to suffer the smell of boiling vinegar through the house and then go for it. It doesn't matter what jars you use for the finished chutney provided they are all scrupulously clean; I recommend a run through with sodium metabisulphite (refer back to Recipe 7). Personally I like to use those French Le Parfait preserving jars. In a way this is overkill, but once they're properly sealed whilst hot, you can be confident they'll keep, and chutney matures well; I have enjoyed a seven-year-old plum chutney. This recipe makes four and a half litres of chutney so you know roughly how many jars to prepare.

INGREDIENTS

500 ml (18 fl oz) distilled malt vinegar

500 ml (18 fl oz) brown malt vinegar

1 kg (2 lb 4 oz) light brown sugar

1.5 kg (3 lb 5 oz) mixed dried fruit

500 g (1 lb 2 oz) fresh garlic

1 kg (2 lb 4 oz) onions

300 g (10½ oz) root ginger

3 kg (6 lb 8 oz) cooking apples

1 kg (2 lb 4 oz) ready soaked dried apricots

100 g (3½ oz) salt

METHOD

Peel the root ginger and slice it, then put it into a food processor with a splash of the vinegar to help it purée and whizz until it is very fine indeed. Scrape it into your preserving pan, which is defined as anything that will hold six litres and is not made of copper. Peel the garlic and whizz it in the food processor with a little more of the vinegar; do not whizz it quite as finely as the ginger. Peel the onions and chop them finely then add them to the pot (you can use the processor for this but you have to be careful that you don't mince them up too finely). Put the dried apricots into the food processor and whizz them with a little vinegar. They need to end up chopped small, but not as small as the garlic, then add them to the pot. Then add everything else and finally the apples, peeled, cored and chopped roughly. Bring the pan to the boil and then simmer away for two hours, without the lid to allow evaporation, stirring every now and then to prevent sticking. All the apple should dissolve and the chutney thicken up nicely. You're aiming to reduce the amount to about four and a half litres. When it is ready to pot, put it into warm, sterilised preserving jars and seal. Keep it for at least two months before trying it. It is worth the wait.

Number Forty-Five – Quiche

In which we query the predilections
of Real Men

From time to time the tide of customers would threaten to engulf the girls serving in the late Peter Pugson's famous cheese shop, and then quick as a flash, one of them would stamp on the floor. In due course, from a door at the rear, Peter himself would appear, blinking mole-like into the light. Behind his shop on the half-landing at the top of the cellar steps was a tiny office where he would sit perched on an upended claret case and use the phone to cajole grudging Frenchmen into better and better deals. From there the stairs led down to a small and immaculate kitchen that was tropically hot even when there was half a metre of snow outside. I would pinch the only stool and enjoy a mug of instant coffee and eclectic conversation whose subject matter ranged freely from Maroilles cheeses, through the excesses of politicians both local and national, to the realms of high opera about which I knew nothing. I would listen and Peter would bake.

Hot French bread, croissants, tarte au fruits, tarte au pommes and quiche. At this point I must confess that I had never been a great fan of quiche. My mother used to make a pretty fair bacon and egg pie, but the whites of the eggs used to go awfully solid. Peter's quiche was a revelation. Pastry, so crisp that it was almost impossible to slice, seemed to combine naturally with a rich filling that seemed barely set. I paid attention during these practical demonstrations, and armed with the knowledge of Peter's secret ingredient – crème fraiche – have been able to develop this quiche recipe of my own. This is not the cold, limp and indigestible wedge that ruins so many fork buffets, but a hearty dish that should be eaten warm as a meal in itself and certainly should never be seen near a refrigerator. If I were you, I'd keep this dish for those occasions when you are eating as a family. It needs to be cooked and then eaten straight from the oven as it cools down – when it's just a bit hotter than lukewarm. There is no room in this timetable for finesse like being polite to guests, coping with latecomers or enjoying an elaborate preceding course.

Some transatlantic wag once remarked that 'real men don't eat quiche'; this only goes to show that they had obviously not tried one straight from the oven, crisp-based and golden-topped.

INTRODUCTION

Crème fraiche is wonderful stuff. It is slightly thicker than double cream and is produced by a similar process to that which is used to make yoghurt. As an ingredient it offers all the richness of sweet cream, but also a pleasant and balancing acidity. Crème fraiche should not be confused with soured cream. You can find it in most good delicatessens and supermarkets. Get a large tub as it keeps well in a fridge and when used instead of ordinary cream in sauces gives a delightful extra lift.

This quiche recipe also includes bacon. Ideally you will need to find a butcher who cures his own, but failing that at least be sure that he slices his own bacon so that you can get the thicker-than-usual rashers you need.

INGREDIENTS FOR THE PASTRY
250 g (9 oz) plain white flour
150 g (5½ oz) unsalted butter
½ tsp salt
1 large fresh egg
Cold water to mix

METHOD FOR THE PASTRY
I confess I use a food processor, it keeps everything cool and it works! Put in the butter and then whizz whilst you drop in the egg and then the flour. Finally add cold water in small amounts and extremely cautiously. As if by magic the pastry will come together and roll up into a ball. Take it out and let it rest in the refrigerator for at least two hours.

Grease a quiche dish about 25 cm (10 in) in diameter with some further butter. Roll out your pastry and line the dish. The pastry should stand some 1 cm (½ in) above the rim. Press the pastry in so that it is even, and prick the base all over with a fork. Then prepare it for baking blind, by adding a sheet of silicone parchment weighted with some dried beans. Bake at gas mark 6 / 400°F / 200°C for about 15 minutes. Remove and allow to cool down.

INGREDIENTS FOR THE FILLING

275 g (9½ oz) thickly sliced streaky bacon

284 ml carton crème fraiche

2 large fresh eggs plus 2 extra yolks

25 g (1 oz) unsalted butter

Freshly ground black pepper

METHOD FOR THE QUICHE

If you have managed to get hold of some home-cured bacon then you'd be advised to blanch it in boiling water briefly to remove some of the salt. Then proceed as per ordinary thick-cut streaky – take off the rind and cut it across into strips about 2 cm (¾ in) wide, fry them in a little butter until they are beginning to colour. Spread them over the bottom of the quiche and press them in a little. Then beat the crème fraiche, the whole eggs and the yolks together and add two twists of freshly ground black pepper. Pour the mixture into the pastry case gently so as not to float the bacon into a corner and dot the surface with a little butter. Then cook in a moderate oven, gas mark 5 / 375°F / 190°C, for fifteen to twenty minutes. Have a look after ten minutes and if it is colouring too quickly for your liking then shield it with a bit of silicone paper.

Take it from the oven and (when it is still cooling down) enjoy it in as macho a manner as good sense allows.

Number Forty-Six – Atholl Brose

*In which we investigate the longest, dankest
canal tunnel in Britain*

I went on three barging holidays in all. Bachelor affairs in the West
Midlands. We would hire our narrowboat from the Ernie Thomas fleet
and set off; strict rules applied. First we had to complete the whole of
the Three Counties Ring in the week allotted (it was a long enough loop
of canals to make that difficult) and secondly the boat was not allowed
to move during pub opening hours. This second stipulation meant quite
a lot of early rising to make sure we achieved each day's allotted
mileage. It also led to some strange bouts of hectic travel to reach pubs
by opening time, and other stretches where the best canalside pubs
came too thick and fast for our plans – like the afternoon spent
dawdling the few miles between lunch at the Blue Lion in Cheswardine
and an evening at the Anchor at Shebden. The fact that we survived at
all speaks volumes for the resilience of youth. I cooked for the six of us
with the occasional 'guest night' when one of the others would offer up
a special delicacy, like the evening at the Anchor when Jimmy (a bearded
Geordie gent from Ashington) made 'ash. It was absolutely delicious

and consisted of 5 lb (these were pre-metric days) of mashed potato, 2 lb of mashed carrot, 2 lb of mashed swede, 2 lb of onions chopped and fried, and a bottle of Guinness all mashed together with a small tin of corned beef and then 'dried off' in the oven in every flat dish the boat possessed. This was my introduction to 'corned beef 'ash', and very tasty it was too, when taken as the overture to a surfeit of beer.

I impressed them all with Atholl brose. I provided it as breakfast on the morning we went through the Harecastle Tunnel, which was closed soon afterwards due to its increasingly dangerous state of repair. The brose was just the thing to keep out the chill, repel the incipient hangover and provide a firm foundation for the day's adventures.

It's a strange thought, but you give a staple carbohydrate to the Italians and you get wonderful pasta dishes; you give rice to the Chinese and get fried rice; you give potatoes to the Belgians and you get frites; and you give oats to the Scots and get porridge! Perhaps this is another instance of northern melancholia. Atholl brose is how all porridge would be if the Scots were an inherently cheerful people.

In the hotel we always served Atholl brose at about six a.m. on New Year's Day, so that our guests didn't go to bed on an empty stomach. It was always much loved and often had the side effect of rekindling the party until lunchtime.

I have read recipes where Atholl brose is made by squeezing the juice from soaked oats and blending the liquid with honey and whisky, but they hold little appeal as I'm not looking for a cocktail. I prefer something a bit more substantial. My Atholl brose is closer to frumenty and fluffin – two Anglo-Saxon yuletide treats. Frumenty is made with kibbled wheat and rum, and fluffin from barley and brandy. Frumenty is even supposed to cure a nagging wife or a grumpy husband although I have no evidence to support the theory.

INTRODUCTION

Atholl brose is smart porridge, and for porridge you need rolled oats. There is an ever-increasing number of options to choose from. All will work equally well. If you make your brose from the larger rolled oats that have been pre-treated for easy cooking then it will tend to be coarser in texture than if you use a very fine oatmeal – it is all a matter of taste. Similarly, you should enliven your brose with whichever whisky you choose – Irish whiskey is particularly smooth and scented if you don't feel you're being churlish. Local honey from bees rather than from the bulk tanks of a supermarket gives a better flavour, as does real cream.

INGREDIENTS

    1 litre (1¾ pints) whole milk
    175 g (6 oz) fine oatmeal
    1 tsp salt

4 tbs runny honey

200 ml (7 fl oz) double cream

75 ml (3 fl oz) Irish whiskey

METHOD

Put the oatmeal and milk into a large saucepan, preferably one with a thick bottom that has a good record as a non-sticker. Bring it up to the boil slowly, stirring as you do so. Turn the heat down and cook very gently for a further ten minutes. Then add the salt and honey and give it another good stir. After a further fifteen minutes take the brose off the heat and beat in the cream and the whiskey. Serve, eat and feel it warming you through.

Number Forty-Seven – Stuffed Savoy

*In which we make the acquaintance
of last autumn's pig*

It was a dark and stormy night when we finally found the house at which we were supposed to pick up the keys. I knocked on the door and we were beckoned into the kitchen by Martoo herself.

We had borrowed a beautiful farmhouse standing squarely on a hilltop in France beside the River Lot for a holiday, during those dull days between Christmas and the New Year, and Martoo was the neighbour who kept the keys. As she was just sitting down to dinner when we arrived, we were invited to join in.

Martoo's farmhouse was built to the traditional pattern: living was done in the kitchen which was effectively on the first floor – the ground floor being taken up by the cowshed, so that the warmth of the animals drifted upwards through cracks between the floorboards and helped keep the cold at bay. The kitchen rejoiced in an open fire with a wide chimney, three rings linked to gas bottles for cooking on, no hot water supply, and a long farm table and benches.

Both Martoo and the other diner, an extremely old farmhand called

Bernard, kept their outer coats and wellington boots on at all times, which wasn't as drab as it may seem due to Martoo's penchant for wearing half a dozen cardigans topped with a floral housecoat and woolly bobble hat when milking the cows and working around and about the farm. Neither of our hosts spoke any English, so for communication we had to manage with my barbaric French.

I opened the batting with polite enquiries about what they grew on the farm. They had a herd of sleek Friesian cows, I knew, I could see them through the cracks in the floorboards. They kept rabbits, I was informed. There was a vineyard and they made their own wine. An orchard was for making their own cider. 'Do you keep pigs?' I enquired. 'Of course,' came the reply, 'there he is,' and Martoo gestured up the chimney. When you are floundering in a foreign language you are only too ready to presume a misunderstanding, but I dutifully looked up into the inglenook to find that it was true. There was a pig, well at least most of him, hung up to cure in the smoke.

Dinner was amazing. There is a section of French society which has a lifestyle to be envied: they live on or about the brink of self-sufficiency, they appear to pay no taxes, and their days are spent in minimal work, eating, drinking, gossiping, and other more salacious pleasures – though not necessarily in that order. Every night Martoo and Bernard would sit down to the kind of dinner we enjoyed that night. First of all we had to overcome the social stigma of not having our own knives.

Your host provides you with a large spoon and a deep soup plate, which you wipe clean or rinse out with wine between courses, and a small glass which serves for all the various drinks, as a pudding bowl, and then finally as a coffee cup. You bring your own jackknife if you wish to cut anything up. We pleaded ignorance and were lent a couple of pocket-knives which looked as though their last duty might have been trimming the ram's feet.

The meal started with highly flavoured soup containing huge lumps of bread, and home-made cider to drink. Then we moved on to a home-tinned pig's liver pâté (which presumably dated back to the demise of our friend in the chimney). Then the pièce de résistance, a stuffed savoy cabbage the size of a football (by now we had moved on to rugged red wine). Then cheese. Then home-bottled cherries in the farm's own eau de vie. Then coffee and some more of the eau de vie. As S. Pepys would have said, 'And so to bed', except that we still hadn't got the keys we had come for or had a glimpse of the house we were to borrow. It was an exceptional meal, and was distinguished by the fact that everything except the salt and pepper and the coffee came from their own resources. It left me with a lasting love of well-stuffed cabbage.

This recipe for stuffed savoy is a development of Martoo's dish and, though time-consuming to prepare, creates a fine show when you present it at table like a round green football with a wonderful interior.

INTRODUCTION

First of all you need the cabbage that is to be stuffed. Pick a large green savoy cabbage. You need large leaves, and it is going to be cooked for so long that however tough the leaves start out they'll be fine when they're finished. You also need some salty smoky bacon, home-cured for choice. The boiling of the cabbage leaches the seasoning out of the stuffing so this is a rare instance when something unduly salty can be used to good advantage.

Finally there is the question of the cloth you wrap the whole thing up in to cook it. Your first choice is a couple of square metres of butter muslin, but failing that you can get away with using old tea towels; they wash out clean afterwards.

INGREDIENTS

A large savoy cabbage
100 g (3½ oz) boiled white long-grain rice
3 cloves of garlic
3 medium onions
225 g (8 oz) lamb's liver
225 g (8 oz) lamb's kidneys
225 g (8 oz) smoked fat bacon
50 g (2 oz) drained sun-dried tomatoes
50 ml (2 fl oz) good olive oil

50 g (2 oz) unsalted butter

Salt and freshly ground black pepper

METHOD

If you have not already got one, now is the time to get hold of one of those hemispherical colanders. Line it with your muslin and then blanch the outer leaves of your savoy cabbage by putting each into boiling water for thirty seconds and then immediately plunging it into cold water. You will find that the leaves become soft and easy to handle. Cut out the central rib, and put the leaves to one side whilst you prepare the filling. Chop the liver and the bacon by hand into batons 3 cm (1¼ in) long by 5 mm (¼ in) square. Core the kidneys and slice in half, then cut them across to give slices about 5 mm (¼ in) thick. Chop the onions finely. Chop the sun-dried tomatoes into small pieces. Take a large frying pan – a wok is ideal – and put the butter and oil into it, then crush the garlic into it and stir over a gentle heat. Then add the onions and sweat until golden. Then add the liver and kidney and finally the bacon; keep stirring as it cooks. Last of all add the sun-dried tomatoes. Then bearing in mind the size of your colander, which you have to hand, add some of the cooked rice (you are aiming for a quantity of finished stuffing that would just about fill your colander), a generous sprinkle of salt and several turns of freshly ground black pepper – mix well.

Then line the muslin-draped colander with the blanched cabbage leaves, leaving a good 7–8 cm (3 in) hanging over the edge of the colander. Make sure that you overlap the leaves to cover the splits where you removed the ribs. This will end up as the outside of your cabbage and needs to be carefully arranged with no gaps. Then add the filling to halfway up the colander, tamp down well and add an intermediate layer of cabbage leaves. Continue filling to the brim and then fold in the cabbage leaves that are hanging over the edge, and add a further one to seal up the join. The stuffing should now be completely enclosed in leaf. Then bring the muslin in and tie it with string so that you end up with a completely round parcel like an old-fashioned Christmas pudding. Congratulations, your stuffed savoy, is now ready for cooking.

Boil the parcel for two hours. Then take it out, cut away the string and unwrap the cabbage, which you will find holds together surprisingly well; pop it on a serving plate with the sealed end down. Serve it by cutting it into wedges at the table. The long cooking will have helped the flavours to blend, and yet it will still be deliciously moist. Enjoy this dish with a glass of red wine and reflect on how unfair it is that, despite the helpful contribution of global warming, in Britain we do not yet have the climate to grow the red wine grape successfully, and we just cannot make our own.

Number Forty-Eight – Scrambled Eggs

In which we stipulate, 'When you're breaking eggs you don't have to be making an omelette'

The worst scrambled eggs I have ever eaten were at a noisy breakfast party at four o'clock in the morning in a flat Reg Bryson shared with several other Antipodeans in the Munster Road. The breakfast was merely a sideshow to the live televising of the British Lions versus All Blacks rugby International. The scrambled eggs came grey and upright – always a bad sign – cut like a wedge of gâteau from a saucepan filled with four dozen beaten eggs and then subjected to gentle heat until they were burnt on the bottom and solid enough to slice. Thank goodness for tomato sauce. And to make matters worse we came second in the Test.

Some of the best scrambled eggs I ever had weren't strictly scrambled at all. There used to be a little café owned by a Frenchman at the top of Dover Street in London that served scrambled eggs in an iron dish. His method was to stir the eggs together with a good deal of butter in the dish and then put it into a slow oven for five minutes, taking it out when the eggs were on the point of cooking, so ensuring that they arrived at the table exactly at that wonderful loose stage.

I have always been fascinated by those recipes where the whole is greater than the sum of its parts – like scrambled eggs where eggs, cream and butter combine to form a dish that is better than each constituent. In the *Guide to Modern Cookery*, which he worked on between 1898 and 1907, Georges-Auguste Escoffier wrote of scrambled eggs: 'This dish is undoubtedly the finest of all egg-preparations, provided the eggs be not over-cooked, and they be kept soft and creamy.' And to put these sentiments into context, they are to be found in his voluminous section about eggs which offers 143 different 'egg-preparations'! I agree with him. Though not, I have to say, with his recipe, which suggests cooking the eggs by themselves and then beating in a lot of butter just prior to serving.

Scrambled eggs are the triumph of timing over everything else; they need to be cooked just so far and no further. For those people who have an inordinate amount of time to spend, and whose fear of potential failure weighs heavy on them, there is always the easy option – the bain-marie. How much nicer, however, to err on the side of bravura and go for it over an open flame. As you gain experience and gradually get the measure of the cooking process it may still on occasion go wrong, forcing you to endure the odd plate of over-solid eggs, but that's a small price easily paid in these days of nicer, more natural tomato sauces.

INTRODUCTION

Let us take sides in the great egg controversy. If you are lucky enough to have your own hens you will feel smugness welling up at this point. Take a proper, day-old egg from a chicken that has wandered about in the paddock. Crack it on to a plate. Note the lack of the air gap that you are accustomed to with supermarket eggs. Perhaps there's the spot that indicates a cockerel has been about his business and your egg is fertile. See how the white 'sits up', and doesn't spread limply across the surface. If you choose to poach it, perhaps for the first time you will see a good-looking poached egg that's been cooked the old-fashioned way freely in boiling water; it'll have some shape to it, holding together rather than drifting as a flobby, watery cloud. And however you choose to cook it, your egg will taste good. Very good indeed. That's because of the roadside gravel, the woodlice, that big worm from the dung heap, and those pot-peelings – in fact everything the hen had to eat. You can tell this by looking at the yolk which will be a different shade from those of mass-produced eggs when the hens are fed artificial colours in their 'layer's mash'. And you can tell with your eyes shut, by tasting the richness of an egg that comes from a hen that has not been fed man-made rations which include every kind of protein imaginable and quite a few that are not.

Please do not think that I am making a passionate statement against modern farming. Good food is good food wherever it comes from. What

I do suggest is that you go out of your way to get hold of the best eggs you possibly can, and that your efforts will be rewarded on the plate. Particularly when you perfect your scrambled eggs.

INGREDIENTS

6 large fresh eggs

50 g (2 oz) best unsalted butter

75 ml (3 fl oz) double cream

Salt and freshly ground black pepper

METHOD

The secret to getting this right is to remember exactly what you did on previous occasions and learn from that. Only make each mistake once. If you served scrambled eggs every day for a month, by the end of that month you would certainly be bored with Escoffier's favourite but you would also be very good at making them.

Take a pan that conducts the heat well: something thick-bottomed and made from well-tinned copper would be perfection. Melt the butter in it very slowly. Meanwhile, beat the eggs with half the cream; stop beating as soon as the mixture is uniform. Take the pan off the heat and add the egg mixture to the butter. Stir. Put the pan back on the heat and gently cook whilst stirring. With practice you'll spot the moment the eggs are on the point of setting.

Quick as a flash, take the pan away from the heat and stir in the other half of the cream to arrest the cooking process; season with salt and freshly ground black pepper. Be brave with the salt as scrambled eggs can be wishy-washy without the proper seasoning. There you have it, perfect scrambled eggs – or perhaps you don't, in which case I recommend that you work out what went wrong and adapt your method to compensate next time.

Persevere, it is worth it.

Number Forty-Nine – Venison without Cherries

*In which we make a stand alongside the
Sheriff of Nottingham*

Venison has always been a fairly pretentious choice of meat. The Sheriff
of Nottingham would have a much better image today if he had not
been forced into the role of fall guy for Robin of Loxley; and Robin
would have been a beastly baron, like all the rest, but for a little
injudicious poaching of the king's deer.

For some while there has been a cheffy fascination with venison. It is
low in cholesterol; very lean; usually organically produced. What could
be nicer? For me the trouble started with the profusion of recipes that
worked their way over from the Continent. A good many of these dishes
featured morello cherries. Suddenly, where once these ghastly bottled,
tinned and frozen black lumps were only to be found atop the foulest
glop of all – Black Forest gâteau – black cherries were piled high on
every imaginable cut of venison.

It was enough to make you wish for some pretty severe restrictions on
just who could eat venison. Which would be a pity, as venison is very
rewarding to cook. The venison of today is very different in character

from that of even twenty years ago. In the nineteenth century, venison tended to come from red deer – the noble animal in Landseer's *Stag at Bay* – a haunch of which was an imposing piece of meat indeed. It was also hung longer and eaten a good deal riper. Nowadays, if you can find yourself a supplier other than the major supermarkets you can enjoy roe deer, fallow deer, sika and even muntjac. Roe deer is the commonest source of venison outside Scotland. And venison can be very good eating indeed. The only pitfalls that attend are the very features that make it such a healthy option – it is very lean and can therefore prove both tough and dry. There are two answers to that. First, a good marinade will stop the meat from being so tough, and secondly, cooking it in a casserole with a rich sauce will banish dryness. Which is what all the black cherry recipes seek to do and so emphatically fail to achieve.

Venison without cherries is based on a precedent set by the rather unlikely use of chocolate in savoury sauces. This practice has its origins in a Mexican dish of turkey with a bitter chocolate sauce which later crops up in Spain as pigeon in chocolate sauce. Good bitter chocolate is the key to success, it enriches the sauce, gives it a good dark colour and glossy texture and amalgamates so perfectly that you would be hard put to it to name the ingredients by tasting the finished dish without some inside knowledge. The secret ingredient also gives you a sauce that is robust enough in flavour to hold its own with the richness of the venison.

Try the dish out and see for yourself. Anything is better than slathering your venison with the top half of a Black Forest gâteau.

INTRODUCTION

Unless you have pretensions as a poacher, it is best to enquire after venison at your favourite butcher. If you draw a blank, then the major supermarkets stock casserole venison, but only at prices considerably wilder than the deer.

When the recipe stipulates strong bitter beer, any of the richer, more hoppy, 'real-ale' types of supermarket bottled beers will do.

For dark chocolate read any chocolate with over 70-per-cent-cocoa solids (I have devoted some time to chocolate in Recipe 21).

When well-reduced stock is mentioned, the rich stock outlined in Recipe 25 will serve; reduce it until it jellies well and then use about 300 ml (10 fl oz).

INGREDIENTS

2 kg (4 lb 8 oz) lean venison

500 ml (18 fl oz) strong bitter beer

2 sticks of celery

4 medium onions

2 tbs red-wine vinegar

50 ml (2 fl oz) good olive oil

250 ml (9 fl oz) well-reduced, home-made stock
30 g (1 oz) strong dark chocolate
Salt and freshly ground black pepper

METHOD

Cut the venison into chunks and put them in a cold marinade made from a splash of the oil, the vinegar, the beer and the celery plus one of the onions, both chopped finely. Toss to coat each piece of meat and then cover with clingfilm and put in the fridge for twenty-four hours.

For the actual cooking, chop the remaining onions finely and soften them in a frying pan using the remaining oil. Then put them into the bottom of a casserole. Pick the meat out of the marinade and seal each piece in the frying pan. Put them into the casserole once they are done. Strain the marinade through a fine sieve and add it to the casserole. Finally add the jellied stock, and put the casserole into a moderate oven – gas mark 4 / 350°F / 180°C – for an hour and half.

After that time take the casserole out of the oven and turn the oven off. Sieve the casserole, catching all the juice in a saucepan and retaining all the meat in the casserole. Return the casserole of meat to the oven whilst you attend to the gravy.

Boil the gravy fiercely until it is reduced to the consistency you like – I think it should coat the back of a spoon. Then polish the sauce by grating the chocolate and adding it whilst you stir. Now, and only now, should you season the sauce with salt and freshly ground black pepper. When it is to your liking, pour it back over the venison and serve immediately, without cherries.

Number Fifty – Roasting-Tin Syrup Cake

*In which we conclude that Eliza Acton would have
been first in the queue for a food processor*

Isabella Beeton would have been quite lost without Mrs Acton. It is one of the quirks of history that Eliza Acton's book *Modern Cookery for Private Families*, which she published in 1845, does not enjoy the same status as Mrs Beeton's *Household Management*, which was published some fifteen years later. In publishing terms this reflects both the triumph of Ward Lock over Longmans, who took the decision to remove Eliza's book from their list in 1918, and an early example of the crucial importance of marketing. Mrs Beeton is supposed to have only written her book because her publisher husband needed a cookery book to fill out his list.

From these beginnings the Beeton juggernaut has rolled onwards to the present day, as the original book was split up and a separate title published from the material in each section, and then everything was brought together again by a succession of different editors as edition has succeeded edition.

It is much too late for Eliza Acton to get the credit she so richly deserves. Mrs Acton was the first recipe writer to print a summary of the ingredients and method, rather than including those elements longhand within the text. She was the first recipe writer (and in this respect Isabella Beeton did not imitate her) to establish a policy of never publishing a recipe without first trying it out.

Mrs Acton is the writers' cookery writer. Witty, trenchant and accurate, she is devoted to her subject and full of insights that are still valid today. She is just as prone to break rules as to make them, but whatever she suggests is always worth considering because it almost inevitably works, however odd it may appear on first reading.

In her chapter on cakes, she offers an alternative method to creaming butter and sugar together before mixing it with the flour and fruit, which was the recognised technique both then and now. Mrs Acton says – and as usual she is right – that you can melt the butter ever so gently and then, providing it is not actually hot, add it to the mixture a bit at a time; she points out that this is an easier way of doing things (right again!).

I think that if Mrs A had had a food processor and microwave in her kitchen, we would all have benefited from a whole new wave of culinary techniques. The kind of techniques you only get from an unstuffy and creative cook.

It would be nice to think that Mrs Acton would have approved of this roasting-tin syrup cake. It meets all of her criteria. It is very easy to make. It is very good to eat. It is supremely practical. And it reflects the eating styles of the day.

Mrs Acton's cakes were of a different kind, as can be seen from her recipe for the original pound cake – I lb flour, I lb sugar, I lb butter, I lb of eggs. Today this would be seen as a sugar and cholesterol bomb, and Eliza's view is uncannily modern. When talking about cakes in general, she noted, 'More illness is caused by habitual indulgence in the richer and heavier kinds of cakes than could easily be credited by persons who have given no attention to the subject.'

Bake this roasting-tin syrup cake, cut yourself a chunk and then settle down to read Mrs Acton's book. The cake will be good but the book will be even better.

INTRODUCTION

In the method for this recipe I presume that you are the proud owner of a food processor. If this is not the case then you'll have to backtrack and recreate for yourself a convenient way of doing things: cream (or melt) the fat and sugar and so forth . . . Aside from these finer points of the method there is very little that can go awry with this cake.

INGREDIENTS

   450 g (1 lb) plain white flour
   225 g (8 oz) caster sugar
   2 tbs golden syrup
   125 g (4½ oz) butter

2 large fresh eggs

275 g (9½ oz) mixed dried fruit

1 tsp powdered cinnamon

1 tsp ground nutmeg

1 tsp bicarbonate of soda

A little fresh milk

METHOD

Take your trusty food processor. Put in it the sugar, butter, syrup and eggs. Whizz until they're creamed. Add the flour, spices and bicarb. Whizz a little more. Add a little milk and whizz until the mixture is like a stiff Yorkshire pudding batter. Then add the fruit and whizz a tiny bit more (your aim is to distribute the fruit evenly throughout the mixture but not to chop it up too much). Then take your largest roasting tin and butter it well, pour the mixture in, and bake in a pre-heated oven – gas mark 4 / 350°F / 180°C. Look at the cake after about an hour; if it is getting too brown on top cover with a piece of baking parchment. It should be done after about an hour and a half. Cool in the tin for ten minutes and then on a rack.

You'll find this cake as delicious as it is easy to make.

INDEX